IS IT REALLY THIS EASY?

Known for his five-ingredient recipes and "make it anywhere" mentality, internet chef Patrick Zeinali makes cooking entertaining, fun, and above all, easy. His simple recipes and boisterous humor have earned him a devoted online following hungry for his novel creations in the kitchen.

This collection of sweet and savory dishes from Patrick features flavorful concoctions that are—you guessed it—so easy to make. These approachable and uncomplicated recipes will prove to you just how accessible cooking can be, regardless of your skill level in the kitchen. Whether you're looking for a between-meals snack, a delectable dessert, or a simple and quick dinner, you'll find something to satisfy your cravings.

It's So Easy to Make orders up 40 savory recipes, like the crispy Cheese-Stuffed Onion Rings and saucy Lollipop Barbecue Wings, along with 40 sweet recipes, such as the gooey Oreo Molten Cake and the toasted Korean Ice Cream Bar, all made with minimal ingredients for maximum enjoyment. Full of clever shortcuts and techniques for using familiar ingredients in unexpected ways, you'll find inspiration in Patrick's ingenious methods. Try your hand at churros made from Oreo cookies and ketchup-flavored potato chips. Or level up with wild and wacky creations like the Edible Plant, Golf Ball Cake, or Jenga Cake.

Yes, it really is this easy!

IT'S SO EASY TO MAKE

PATRICK ZEINALI
IT'S SO EASY TO MAKE

Snacks, Sweets, and **Quick Eats** for Any Kitchen

PHOTOGRAPHY BY MAX MILLA

Publisher Mike Sanders
Art & Design Director William Thomas
Editorial Director Ann Barton
Editor Brandon Buechley
Senior Designer Jessica Lee
Senior Layout Technician Ayanna Lacey
Illustrator Max Erwin
Photographer Max Milla
Photo Assistant David Peng
Food Stylist Judean Sakimoto
Recipe Testers Lovoni Walker, Diana Kim, and Elle DeBell
Copy Editor Monica Stone
Proofreaders Mira S. Park and Lisa Starnes
Indexer Celia McCoy

First American Edition, 2025
Published in the United States by DK Publishing
1745 Broadway, 20th Floor, New York, NY 10019

The authorized representative in the EEA is Dorling Kindersley Verlag
GmbH. Arnulfstr. 124, 80636 Munich, Germany

Copyright © Patrick Zeinali
DK, a Division of Penguin Random House LLC
25 26 27 28 29 10 9 8 7 6 5 4 3 2 1
001–341397–AUG2025

All rights reserved.
Without limiting the rights under the copyright reserved above, no part of this publication may be reproduced, stored in or introduced into a retrieval system, or transmitted, in any form, or by any means (electronic, mechanical, photocopying, recording, or otherwise), without the prior written permission of the copyright owner.

No part of this publication may be used or reproduced in any manner for the purpose of training artificial intelligence technologies or systems. In accordance with Article 4③ of the DSM Directive 2019/790, DK expressly reserves this work from the text and data mining exception.

A catalog record for this book
is available from the Library of Congress.
ISBN 978-0-5938-4057-3

DK books are available at special discounts when purchased in bulk for sales promotions, premiums, fund-raising, or educational use. For details, contact SpecialSales@dk.com

Printed and bound in Slovakia

www.dk.com

This book was made with Forest Stewardship Council™ certified paper – one small step in DK's commitment to a sustainable future. Learn more at
www.dk.com/uk/information/sustainability

To my dad, Archie Zeinali

You inspired me to become the cook I am today, and even though you're no longer with us, your presence is felt on every page.

Love you.

CONTENTS

Welcome to It's So Easy to Make! 9
My Story 10
Cooking Should Be Fun and Easy 13
Essential Equipment 14
Pantry Staples 17

APPETIZERS, FINGER FOODS & MORE

Cheese Balls 21
Cheese-Stuffed Onion Rings 22
Homemade Cream Cheese 25
Crispy Potato Rings 26
Cheetos-Seasoned Chips 29
Crispy Garlic-Butter Fries 30
Cheese-Stuffed Chicken Nuggets 32
Microwave Potato Chips 35
Chicken Rings 37
Homemade "Mozzarella" Cheese 38
Microwave Mug Pizza 41
Onion Rings 42
Potato Boat 45
Sriracha-Honey Chicken Nuggets 46
Fully Loaded Nachos 49
Pizza in a Pan 50
Ketchup Chips 53
Cheese Donuts 54
Scalloped Potatoes 57
Potato Cheese Sticks 58

MAINS, SIDES & BREADS

Tender Beef Short Ribs 63
Street Tacos 64
Honey-Butter Fried Chicken 66
Orange Chicken 68
Cheese-Stuffed Bread 71
Bubble Shrimp 72
Lule Kabobs 75
Lemon-Pepper Wings 76
Mac & Cheese 79
Pan Bread 80
Fall-Off-the-Bone Barbecue Ribs 83
Cheese-Stuffed Flatbreads 84
3-Ingredient Flour Tortillas 87
Smash Burger 88
Spicy Peanut Noodles 91
Lollipop Barbecue Wings 92
Hot Wings 95
Garlic Noodles 96
Fall-Off-the-Bone Beef Ribs 99
Chicharrones 100

CAKES, PIES & SWEET BREADS

Cake Pops 105
Monkey Bread 106
Mini Cheesecake Cups 109
Coffee-Chocolate Pudding Cake 110

Oreo Molten Cake	113
Japanese Fluffy Cake	114
Tiny Pancakes	117
Nutella Brioche	118
Jenga Cake	121
Éclair Cake	122
Golf Ball Cake	125
One-Pan Chocolate Cake	126
Oreo Cake	129
Sponge Cake	130
Spiral Croissants	133
Japanese Stuffed Pancakes	134
Fluffy Pancake	137
Donut Holes with Caramel	138
Chocolate Donuts	141
Chocolate Cake with Chocolate Bar	143

DESSERT CUPS, ICE CREAMS, CHOCOLATE & MORE

Oreo Cream Cups	147
Chocolate from Scratch	148
Tiramisu Cups	151
Chocolate Chip Cookie Cup	152
Jelly Roll-Ups	155
Edible Plant	156
Brownie in a Cup	159
3-Ingredient Peanut Butter Cup Fudge	160

Chocolate Ganache Brownies	163
Marshmallow Chocolate Bar	164
Dessert Burrito	167
Chocolate Brownie Dish	168
Oreo Ice Cream Bar	171
Korean Ice Cream Bar	172
Edible Chocolate Chip Cookie Dough	175
Cookies and Cream Churros	176
Oreo Ice Cream Sandwich	179
Chocolate Cream Cups	180
Tiramisu	183
Homemade Ice Cream	184
Index	186
Acknowledgments	191

WELCOME TO IT'S SO EASY TO MAKE

First off, thank you so much for reading this cookbook. Out of the millions of cookbooks out there, you chose mine, and I appreciate that more than you know.

This book is written for cooks of all skill levels and especially for those who want to get in the kitchen but feel overwhelmed by all the information out there. I created this book not only because I love cooking but because I love making *simple, delicious*, and—most importantly—*easy* recipes.

When I first started cooking, I used to follow recipes from professional chefs and home cooks. The one thing that turned me off was how many ingredients and steps it took to make just one dish. I remember spending three hours cooking a meal, enjoying it for only ten minutes, and then spending another hour cleaning up. That process would turn anyone off, and it did me—until I realized that delicious meals don't need to be complicated.

So I started finding shortcuts to make some of my favorite meals and *boom!* Everything changed. This book is designed for easy cooking, and one thing you'll notice right away is that most recipes have only a handful of ingredients. I don't want you running to the store to buy a ton of things you'll only use once. In fact, many of the ingredients in this book are used repeatedly, so you'll get the most out of every purchase.

Some of you might know me from my five ingredients or less cooking videos online. A lot of people think I make those just for the internet, but as my friends will tell you, I actually live by that rule. I spend no more than 1 hour in the kitchen—and that includes cooking, cleaning, and eating. As much as I love cooking, I want to be in and out of the kitchen as quickly as possible!

This book focuses equally on many of my favorite savory recipes and sweet recipes. I want you, the reader, to get as much as you can out of this book, and what better way to do that than to offer a wide variety? When you think of sweet recipes, one word probably comes to mind: *baking*. I love to bake just as much as I love to cook. There's a science to baking, and it feels so rewarding when you get it right. But don't worry—all the baking recipes in this book are designed to be super simple too.

Another reason I wanted to include a diverse assortment of recipes is because we all like different things, to put it simply. And I believe there is a quick-and-easy recipe in these pages for everyone. By the time you're done with this book, I'm confident you'll not only fall in love with cooking but you'll also be ready to impress all your friends and family in the kitchen.

MY STORY

My obsession with cooking started when I was just a little kid. I remember sitting on the corner of my parents' bed with my dad and watching Emeril Lagasse—a renowned American chef and TV personality with a hugely successful cooking show. Every time Emeril went to season something with salt, he'd say his catchphrase—Bam!—and toss the salt. The live audience would erupt in claps and cheers, and so would my dad and I.

I have an embarrassing memory: Whenever I was in the kitchen as a kid, making my favorite dish, usually a hamburger with french fries, I'd pretend I was on a cooking show, explaining what I was doing step-by-step. And now I do just that for a living. Life is crazy sometimes.

My dad was the cook in our family. He made the best Persian and Italian food I've ever had. Anytime he was in the kitchen, I was right there with him, acting as his sous-chef. He taught me a lot of the cooking techniques I still use to this day, and his obsession and passion for cooking definitely rubbed off on me.

A lot of my success today comes from the risks my dad took in life. As an immigrant parent, he was a hard worker who never backed down when things got tough. I remember when he wanted to open an Italian café in Westwood, California, right next to UCLA, the landlord told him, "Sir, you know there are three other prominent Italian restaurants nearby. Are you sure you want to open one here?" And my dad, with his Persian accent, confidently replied, "Why not?" He believed in his food so much that failure wasn't an option—and he didn't fail. His café became one of the most successful spots in the area, running for over ten years. People even told my dad his Italian food was the best in town.

Dad's confidence taught me something: In life, you have to take risks to be successful. The only time you truly fail is when you stop chasing what you want.

This career didn't come to me on a silver platter. There were a lot of ups and downs. For a while, I wanted to be a musician. I played drums for many years and was part of a few music groups trying to break into the industry. After eight grueling years, things were not looking good. But I didn't let that stop me from being creative. I reverted to my roots—cooking.

For three years, I invested almost all my money into the videos I was making, pushing through uncertainty. Finally, I was able to turn my dreams into reality. And it all started with a love for cooking, followed by a lot of hard work combined with the lessons I learned from my dad.

COOKING SHOULD BE FUN AND EASY

One of the main reasons this cookbook exists is because I truly believe cooking shouldn't feel overwhelming. I've heard countless stories from people I've met throughout my life about how stepping into the kitchen to cook a delicious meal—or even just a dessert—feels daunting. One of the most common things I hear is: *When I see a recipe with a long ingredient list, I immediately give up.* Honestly, I get it—I feel the same way sometimes.

I've seen this happen again and again with my friends, my family, and even myself. When we get excited about something new—whether it's going to the gym, learning to draw, or trying out cooking—we often dive in too hard and fast. The excitement fizzles out and we give up because the process feels too overwhelming. Most of us want cooking to be fun and *easy* because we're all juggling so much in our daily lives, and spending endless hours in the kitchen just isn't realistic.

That's why this book is all about taking it slow, having fun, and easing into the kitchen. Think of it as the starting point for your cooking journey. We'll start with simple, approachable recipes, and as the book progresses, we'll build up to more advanced techniques. By the time you're done, you'll feel confident enough to tackle even the most challenging recipes out there. But most importantly, we'll make sure you enjoy the process.

I want this book to be fun and approachable, not overly serious or intimidating. It's designed for everyone, no matter your skill level. This is the beginning of your journey as a home cook, and I truly believe you'll walk away from this book as a better cook, armed with skills that will stay with you for life.

ESSENTIAL EQUIPMENT

No matter how easy these recipes might be to make, they still require top-notch equipment. To master your skills and the recipes in this book, I recommend having your kitchen prepped and ready with these essential tools.

COOKING VESSELS

- ❏ Baking sheets
- ❏ Dutch oven or deep pot
- ❏ Medium and large saucepans
- ❏ Nonstick frying pan

UTENSILS

- ❏ Heatproof tongs
- ❏ Knife set
- ❏ Measuring cups and spoons
- ❏ Skewers (metal or bamboo)
- ❏ Slotted spoon
- ❏ Spatula
- ❏ Whisk

APPLIANCES

- ❏ Food processor
- ❏ Hand mixer
- ❏ High-speed blender
- ❏ Oven with broiler

OTHER TOOLS

- ❏ Candy/deep-fry thermometer
- ❏ Cheesecloth
- ❏ Colander
- ❏ Cutting board
- ❏ Mixing bowls
- ❏ Parchment paper
- ❏ Rolling pin
- ❏ Sieve/strainer
- ❏ Wire rack

PANTRY STAPLES

Quality dishes call for quality ingredients. These recipes are packed with accessible ingredients you can find at your local grocery store without any problem. Be sure to keep your pantry stocked with these crucial components.

DRY GOODS

- ❏ Active dry yeast
- ❏ All-purpose flour
- ❏ Baking powder
- ❏ Baking soda
- ❏ Breadcrumbs
- ❏ Cornstarch
- ❏ Sugar (granulated, brown)

MEAT AND DAIRY

- ❏ Butter
- ❏ Cheese (mozzarella, cheddar, Parmesan)
- ❏ Chicken (breast, ground)
- ❏ Eggs
- ❏ Milk (whole)
- ❏ Sour cream

SEASONINGS

- ❏ Black pepper
- ❏ Chili powder
- ❏ Garlic powder
- ❏ Onion powder
- ❏ Paprika
- ❏ Salt

OTHER

- ❏ Barbecue sauce
- ❏ Frying oil (vegetable, canola, peanut)
- ❏ Lemon juice
- ❏ Olive oil
- ❏ Potatoes (russet)
- ❏ Soy sauce
- ❏ Vinegar (white, apple cider)

APPETIZERS, FINGER FOODS & MORE

CHEESE BALLS

PREP TIME: 15 MINUTES, PLUS 5 MINUTES TO COOL • **COOK TIME:** 5 MINUTES

This gooey recipe will give cheese lovers something to rave about. It only requires five ingredients to make it, and it will definitely leave you wanting more. I came up with this recipe while in a pinch to prepare some quick appetizers for my guests. I wanted this recipe to be so easy that even my 5-year-old nephew could make it!

MAKES 6 CHEESE BALLS

1 cup milk

⅔ cup all-purpose flour, plus more for work surface and kneading

1 teaspoon salt

One 4-ounce (113g) block low-moisture mozzarella cheese (see Note)

3 cups frying oil

SPECIAL EQUIPMENT

Candy/deep-fry thermometer

1. Add the milk to a medium saucepan over medium-low heat. Bring the milk to a gentle boil.

2. Add the flour and salt to the milk and then remove the saucepan from the heat. Mix until a dough forms. Set the dough aside to cool for about 5 minutes.

3. Lightly flour a work surface and, using your hands, knead the cooled dough on the floured surface until softened, about 2 minutes.

4. Slice the cheese into 6 cubes of equal size.

5. Cut the dough into 6 equal-size pieces. Using your hands, flatten each piece of dough and place a cheese cube on top. Close the dough around each cheese cube and use your hands to roll it into a ball.

6. Pour the frying oil into a medium saucepan and place over medium heat. Heat the oil to 325°F (165°C), using a deep-fry thermometer to measure the temperature.

7. Fry the cheese balls in the hot oil, until all the sides are golden brown, 3 to 5 minutes. Using a slotted spoon, transfer the cheese balls to a plate lined with paper towels and serve immediately.

NOTE

Any type of cheese works for this recipe. Just be sure to use a block of cheese so you can cube it as instructed.

CHEESE-STUFFED ONION RINGS

PREP TIME: 15 MINUTES • **COOK TIME:** 15 MINUTES

Yes, traditional onion rings are delicious, but this recipe levels them up by stuffing them with delicious cheese! Like many of you, I am a huge fan of cheese, and if there is a moment where I can add cheese to a savory dish, I won't hesitate.

MAKES 8 RINGS

2 large white onions

One 4-ounce (113g) block low-moisture mozzarella cheese

½ cup all-purpose flour

1 cup breadcrumbs

2 large eggs

2 cups frying oil

Salt, to taste

SPECIAL EQUIPMENT

Candy/deep-fry thermometer

1. Peel and cut the onions into about 1-inch (2.5cm) thick rings. Separate the rings.

2. Slice the mozzarella into strips that are about 1-inch (2.5cm) thick, the same as the onion rings.

3. Place a smaller onion ring inside a larger onion ring, leaving a small gap between them.

4. Fill the gap between the onion rings with the mozzarella strips until the entire gap is filled with cheese.

5. Place the flour and breadcrumbs each into a separate shallow bowl. Crack the eggs into a small dish or ramekin and then beat them until scrambled.

6. Place a prepared onion ring in the flour. Then dip the ring in the eggs. Finally, coat the ring in breadcrumbs. It may take two rounds to fully coat the rings.

7. Add the frying oil to a medium pot and place it over medium heat. Heat the frying oil to 325°F (165°C), using a deep-fry thermometer to measure the temperature.

8. Working in batches, fry the onion rings until golden brown, 3 to 5 minutes and then, using a slotted spoon, transfer the onion rings from the oil to a serving dish lined with paper towels. Salt them to taste and serve immediately.

HOMEMADE CREAM CHEESE

PREP TIME: 30 MINUTES, PLUS 4 HOURS TO CHILL • **COOK TIME:** 20 MINUTES

I've always been curious if homemade cheese would be better than the store-bought stuff, and the answer is a resounding yes! By leaving out a lot of the shelf-stable ingredients like sorbic acid, sodium phosphate, cellulose powder, etc., you truly taste the natural richness of the cheese. This homemade cream cheese recipe only requires a few ingredients and is probably one of the easiest cheeses to make.

MAKES 1 CUP

½ gallon (1.89L) whole milk
½ cup lemon juice
½ teaspoon salt
¼ cup reserved whey (milk water), plus more if needed

SPECIAL EQUIPMENT

Sieve or strainer
Cheesecloth
High-speed blender

1. Line a large sieve with cheesecloth and place it over a large bowl. Set aside.
2. Place a large pot over medium-low heat, add the milk, and bring it to a boil. As soon as it begins boiling, turn off the heat.
3. Add the lemon juice to the hot milk and gently stir. Continue stirring until curds form.
4. Once cheese curds form, gently ladle or pour the curds into the cheesecloth-lined sieve. Allow the curds to drain for 20 to 30 minutes. Reserve the drained whey (milk water) for the next step.
5. Add the drained cheese curds and salt to a blender. Slowly pour in the ¼ cup reserved whey, blending as you go. Add additional whey until you reach your desired consistency.
6. Transfer the cheese to a bowl and cover it with a lid or plastic wrap.
7. Store the cream cheese in the fridge for at least 4 hours before using. The cream cheese can be stored in an airtight container in the fridge for 7 to 10 days.

VARIATION

You can use any acid that you prefer, such as lime juice or vinegar, instead of the lemon juice.

CRISPY POTATO RINGS

PREP TIME: 10 MINUTES • **COOK TIME:** 15 MINUTES

We've all had onion rings before, but this recipe is a twist on that, swapping potatoes for onions. These are crunchy on the outside, but soft and creamy on the inside, thanks to my method of boiling and mashing. Give this fun recipe a try—you'll love it!

MAKES 5-6 RINGS

1 large russet potato

¼ cup cornstarch, plus more for work surface

1 teaspoon salt

1 tablespoon chopped fresh parsley

2 cups frying oil

SPECIAL EQUIPMENT

Rolling pin

2½-inch (6.5cm) and 1¼-inch (3cm) cookie cutters

Candy/deep-fry thermometer

1. Peel the potato and roughly chop it into pieces.
2. Add water and the chopped potatoes to a medium pot, ensuring the potatoes are well covered and have space. Place the pot over medium heat and boil until the potatoes are soft and fork-tender, about 10 minutes.
3. Drain potatoes, place them in a medium bowl, and mash well with a potato masher or a fork. Add the cornstarch, salt, and parsley to the mashed potatoes. Mix well until it forms a dough-like consistency.
4. Transfer the mixture to a work surface lightly dusted with cornstarch and, using a rolling pin, roll it out into a layer about ¼-inch (6.5mm) thick.
5. Using the medium and small round cookie cutters, cut rings out of the mixture. Start by pressing down with the medium cookie cutter and then pressing the smaller one inside that. Remove both cutters and peel away the potato-mixture ring. You should have enough of the mixture to cut 5 or 6 rings total.
6. Add the frying oil to a a medium pot and place it over medium heat. Heat the frying oil to 350°F (180°C), using a deep-fry thermometer to measure the temperature.
7. Fry the potato rings until golden brown, 4 to 8 minutes. Serve immediately.

CHEETOS-SEASONED CHIPS

PREP TIME: 20 MINUTES • **COOK TIME:** 20 MINUTES

Cheetos were my childhood snack. I always got them during my school lunches to help disguise the horrible-tasting cafeteria food. I wanted to make Cheetos at home, but it's difficult to replicate the puff shape. Instead, I came up with these crinkle-cut potato chips seasoned with Cheetos powder. Making homemade chips is the best because you see the ingredients that go into them, and you can control the amount of seasoning!

MAKES 1 BATCH

3 large russet potatoes

2 cups frying oil

2 tablespoons Cheetos powder (see Note)

SPECIAL EQUIPMENT

Mandoline or crinkle-cut tool

Candy/deep-fry thermometer

1. Peel the potatoes and slice them thinly using a mandoline.
2. Place a medium pot filled halfway with water over high heat and bring to a boil.
3. Add the sliced potatoes to the pot and boil for 5 minutes.
4. Using a slotted spoon, remove the potatoes from the pot and place them on a plate lined with paper towels. Pat them dry with paper towels.
5. Add the frying oil to a medium pot over medium heat. Heat the frying oil to 350°F (180°C), using a deep-fry thermometer to measure the temperature.
6. Working in batches, fry the potatoes in the hot oil until golden brown, 5 to 8 minutes.
7. Transfer the fried potato chips to a medium bowl and add the Cheetos powder, mixing well until the chips are coated evenly with the powder.
8. Serve the chips as is or alongside your preferred dipping sauce.

NOTE

You can purchase the Cheetos powder online, or as I tend to do, you can use the packet included in a box of Cheetos Mac 'n Cheese.

VARIATION

If you prefer different seasonings, feel free to get creative and swap out the Cheetos powder with another, such as salt and pepper, paprika, lemon-pepper seasoning blend, etc.

CRISPY GARLIC-BUTTER FRIES

PREP TIME: 30 MINUTES • **COOK TIME:** 20 MINUTES

These fries are the perfect side dish for any meal, combining crispy potatoes with rich, savory flavors. As a garlic lover, I just knew that mixing butter and garlic with French fries would create a creamy umami flavor that is simply out of this world. I also love how soft the middle part of the french fry is, thanks to the cornstarch we add to the potatoes.

MAKES 3 SERVINGS

3 large russet potatoes
2 tablespoons cornstarch
1 teaspoon coarse salt
2 cups frying oil
2 tablespoons butter
4 garlic cloves, minced
Fresh chopped parsley, for garnish

SPECIAL EQUIPMENT
Candy/deep-fry thermometer

1. Peel and cut the potatoes into ¼-inch (6.5mm) thick french-fry shapes.
2. Soak the cut potatoes in cold water for a few minutes to remove all the starch.
3. Fill a medium pot with 3 cups of water and bring to a boil over high heat.
4. Add the fries to the pot in batches and boil each batch for 3 to 4 minutes.
5. Remove the fries from the pot and pat them dry with paper towels.
6. Place the fries into a large bowl and add the cornstarch and salt, tossing the fries until fully coated.
7. Add the frying oil to a medium pot over medium heat. Bring the oil to 350°F (180°C), using a deep-fry thermometer to measure the temperature.
8. Fry the potatoes until golden brown, 5 to 8 minutes, and set aside on a plate lined with paper towels to drain.
9. For the garlic-butter sauce, place a large, deep pan over low heat and add the butter and garlic, stirring until fully melted and combined.
10. Add the drained fries to the large pan and toss well until fully coated in garlic butter.
11. Garnish with parsley and enjoy.

CHEESE-STUFFED CHICKEN NUGGETS

PREP TIME: 20 MINUTES, PLUS 30 MINUTES TO CHILL • **COOK TIME:** 10 MINUTES

We've all had chicken nuggets growing up and even into adulthood. (Don't lie, you know you love a good McDonald's chicken nugget.) Well, what if we added cheese right in the middle of them? This recipe will show you how to do just that. It's also super easy to make and tastes as amazing as you can imagine.

MAKES 8 NUGGETS

1 pound (454g) ground chicken
2 tablespoons mayonnaise
1 teaspoon salt
1 teaspoon garlic powder
One 4-ounce (113g) block low-moisture mozzarella cheese
½ cup all-purpose flour
1 large egg
¼ cup water
2 cups frying oil
1 cup breadcrumbs

SPECIAL EQUIPMENT
Candy/deep-fry thermometer

1. In a medium bowl, mix the ground chicken, mayo, salt, and garlic powder. Set aside.
2. Divide the chicken mixture into 8 equal portions, place them on a plate or baking sheet and chill in the fridge for 30 minutes.
3. Cut the mozzarella cheese block into eight ½-inch (1.25cm) cubes.
4. Remove the chicken from the fridge and flatten a portion with your hands. Place a cheese cube on top, close the chicken mixture around the cheese, and roll it into a ball. Place it back on the plate and repeat the process with the remaining portions.
5. In a medium bowl, mix the flour, egg, and water to form a batter. Add the breadcrumbs to a shallow dish.
6. Pour the frying oil into a medium saucepan and heat to 300°F (150°C), using a deep-fry thermometer to measure the temperature.
7. While the oil heats, dip each chicken ball in the batter until fully coated. Transfer it to the breadcrumbs and roll until fully coated with the crumbs. Place on a plate or wire rack. Repeat with the remaining chicken balls.
8. Fry the chicken balls for 3 to 5 minutes.
9. Leaving the chicken balls in the pan, increase the temperature of the oil to 350°F (180°C) and continue to fry them until golden brown and an internal temperature of 165°F (74°C) is reached, 1 to 2 additional minutes. Serve immediately.

MICROWAVE POTATO CHIPS

PREP TIME: 10 MINUTES • **COOK TIME:** 8 MINUTES

Say goodbye to the frying pan, frying oil, lengthy processes, and headache of making potato chips because this recipe is probably the easiest in the entire book. You most likely have all the equipment and ingredients to make these chips right now. I make this recipe often because it's delicious, easy, and best of all, healthy!

MAKES 2-3 SERVINGS

- 2 large russet potatoes
- 2 tablespoons olive oil
- Salt, to taste

1. Thinly slice the potatoes into chip shapes.
2. Soak the slices in ice-cold water for 5 minutes to remove the starch. Drain the water.
3. Pat the potato slices dry with paper towels, place them on a microwave-safe plate lined with parchment paper, and brush both sides of the potato slices with olive oil.
4. Place the plate in the microwave and cook for 3 to 4 minutes, then flip and cook for 3 to 4 additional minutes until brown and crispy (see Note). Salt to taste and enjoy!

NOTE

The cook time will vary depending on your microwave wattage. In my 1600-watt microwave, this recipe takes 6 minutes. A lower-wattage microwave might require up to 12 minutes.

CHICKEN RINGS

PREP TIME: 45 MINUTES, PLUS 2 HOURS TO FREEZE • **COOK TIME:** 1 HOUR

You might think that ring formations are only for onions, but you've just discovered the next best thing, and it's made of chicken. The best part about this recipe is that it's not just chicken; you mix it with potatoes and breadcrumbs, which give it a creamier texture with a crunchy outside shell.

MAKES 6-8 RINGS

1 pound (454g) ground chicken

1 small russet potato, boiled and mashed

4 tablespoons breadcrumbs

1 pinch salt

2 cups all-purpose flour, divided

1 cup milk

2 large eggs

½ cup cornstarch

3 cups frying oil

SPECIAL EQUIPMENT

Candy/deep-fry thermometer

1. Combine the ground chicken, mashed potato, breadcrumbs, and salt in a medium bowl.

2. Place the chicken mixture in a piping bag or sealable plastic bag with the corner cut away for piping.

3. Line a baking sheet with parchment paper and pipe the mixture into rings on the parchment paper. You should be able to create 6 to 8 rings depending on the size of your baking sheet.

4. Transfer the baking sheet to the freezer until the chicken rings have fully frozen, about 2 hours.

5. Prepare two separate small bowls. In one bowl, mix together 1 cup flour, the milk, and the eggs until you have a pancake batter consistency. In the other bowl, mix together the remaining 1 cup flour and the cornstarch.

6. Remove the chicken from the freezer and toss the frozen chicken rings in the flour-cornstarch mixture, then in the batter, and back into the flour-cornstarch mixture until fully coated.

7. Add the frying oil to a medium pot and place it over medium heat. Bring the oil to 325°F (165°C), using a deep-fry thermometer to measure the temperature.

8. Fry the chicken rings one at a time until golden brown and crispy, 5 to 8 minutes. Transfer the rings to a plate lined with paper towels and let cool slightly before serving.

HOMEMADE "MOZZARELLA" CHEESE

PREP TIME: 10 MINUTES, PLUS 5 HOURS TO CHILL • **COOK TIME:** 20 MINUTES

Homemade anything always tastes better, and this mozzarella-like cheese is no exception. While it's not the traditional way of making mozzarella, it's definitely better than much of the cheese you buy at the store. It doesn't contain all those weird additives that alter the flavor. Plus, it's super easy, fun, and satisfying to make.

MAKES 1 BLOCK

½ gallon (1.89L) plus ⅓ cup whole milk, divided

10 tablespoons white vinegar, divided

1 teaspoon baking soda

1 tablespoon water

4 tablespoons butter

SPECIAL EQUIPMENT

Sieve or strainer

High-speed blender

1. Place a large pot over low heat, add the ½ gallon milk, and heat until lukewarm.
2. Pour 5 tablespoons vinegar into the milk and gently mix until cheese curds form. Remove from the heat.
3. Using a sieve, drain the liquid and curds to extract the cheese curds and discard the liquid. Squeeze and mold the curds to form a ball. Set aside.
4. Fit a small pot with a medium nonreactive metal or heatproof glass bowl; the bowl shouldn't touch the bottom of the pot but should sit in the top half of the pot. Set the bowl aside. Fill the pot halfway with water and place over medium heat to boil.
5. Meanwhile, in a small bowl, mix the remaining 5 tablespoons vinegar with the baking soda and water. Pour this mixture into a blender.
6. Add the cheese-curd ball, the remaining ⅓ cup milk, and the butter to the blender and blend on high until fully smooth.
7. Place the blended mixture into the medium nonreactive metal or heatproof glass bowl and set it over the small pot of boiling water. Stir for about 10 minutes, until the mixture thins out slightly.
8. Transfer the cheese mixture to a lightly greased container, cover, and place it in the fridge to cool for at least 5 hours.
9. Once cooled, slice the cheese into pieces and use as desired.
10. The mozzarella can be stored in an airtight container in the fridge for up to 7 days.

MICROWAVE MUG PIZZA

PREP TIME: 5 MINUTES • **COOK TIME:** 2 MINUTES

This is one of those recipes I made during a late-night craving after opening and closing my fridge a hundred times, hoping food would somehow magically appear. I love pizza, but I didn't want to spend forever making the dough and letting it proof; I wanted something quick and easy. This recipe doesn't even involve an oven—just 2 minutes in the microwave, and you're eating some delicious pizza!

MAKES 1 SERVING

- ¼ cup all-purpose flour
- ⅛ teaspoon baking powder
- 1/16 teaspoon baking soda
- Pinch of salt
- 3 tablespoons milk
- 1 tablespoon olive oil
- 1½ tablespoons pizza sauce
- 2 tablespoons shredded mozzarella cheese
- 2 slices pepperoni, quartered (see Note) or 8 small pepperoni rounds

1. Combine the flour, baking powder, baking soda, and salt in a large 20-ounce (600ml) mug, and mix until well combined.

2. Add the milk and olive oil and continue mixing until a batter forms. Scrape down the sides of the mug to ensure all the batter is on the bottom.

3. Gently add the pizza sauce on top of the batter, followed by the mozzarella cheese and pepperoni, or any other toppings you prefer.

4. Place the mug in the microwave and cook for 1 to 2 minutes. Be sure to check on it every 30 seconds to ensure it is properly cooked through.

NOTE
I often use a small pizza cutter to cut slices of pepperoni into smaller pieces for this recipe.

ONION RINGS

PREP TIME: 15 MINUTES • **COOK TIME:** 12 MINUTES

Onion rings are an underrated side item for a good burger. Of course, everyone loves a side of French fries with their burger or any other fast-food item, but there's nothing like well-made onion rings, and this recipe delivers just that. There are many approaches to making onion rings, but as with the rest of this book, we'll take the easiest route without sacrificing flavor.

MAKES 2 SERVINGS

2 large white onions

2 cups all-purpose flour, divided

½ cup cornstarch

1 teaspoon salt

1 teaspoon black pepper

1 cup plus 3 tablespoons ice-cold water

3 cups panko breadcrumbs

3 cups frying oil

SPECIAL EQUIPMENT

Candy/deep-fry thermometer

1. Slice the onions into rings.
2. In a small bowl, mix 1 cup flour together with the cornstarch, salt, black pepper, and water until well combined.
3. Add the remaining 1 cup flour to a shallow bowl. Add the breadcrumbs to a second shallow bowl.
4. Add the frying oil to a medium pot and place over medium heat. Bring the oil to 350°F (180°C), using a deep-fry thermometer to measure the temperature.
5. Toss the onion rings in the flour, then dip in the wet batter, and finally coat in the breadcrumbs.
6. Working in batches, fry the onion rings in the hot oil until golden brown and crispy, 3 to 5 minutes each batch.
7. Transfer the fried onion rings to a plate lined with paper towels to cool slightly before serving.

POTATO BOAT

PREP TIME: 10 MINUTES • **COOK TIME:** 1 HOUR AND 10 MINUTES

When I was in middle school, the cafeteria sold these things called potato boats during lunchtime. Cheesy, soft, creamy, and just satisfying, they were probably the only delicious item served at my school's cafeteria. I haven't been able to find anything like them anywhere, so I decided to make my own.

MAKES 3 SERVINGS

- 3 medium Yukon Gold or russet potatoes
- 2 teaspoons olive oil
- ¼ cup milk
- 1 cup cheddar cheese, divided
- 1 tablespoon chopped fresh parsley, plus more for garnish (optional)
- Salt, to taste
- Chopped fresh chives, for garnish (optional)

1. Preheat the oven to 375°F (190°C).
2. Massage the potatoes with the olive oil and place them on a baking sheet lined with parchment paper. Bake for 1 hour or until soft. Remove from the oven and let cool slightly. Leave the oven on.
3. Cut off the top of the potatoes lengthwise and carefully scoop out the flesh into a medium bowl, leaving about ½ inch (1.25cm) of potato flesh attached to the skins. Set aside the potato boats. Discard the tops after removing the flesh.
4. Add the milk, ¾ cup cheddar cheese, and parsley to the bowl of scooped-out potato flesh. Mix well.
5. Spoon equal portions of the cheese-potato mixture back into the potato boats, adding the remaining ¼ cup cheddar cheese over the tops in equal portions.
6. Place the potato boats back on the lined baking sheet and return it to the oven for about 3 minutes, until the cheese has fully melted and browned a little on top.
7. Season with salt, garnish with chopped parsley or chives if using, and serve.

SRIRACHA-HONEY CHICKEN NUGGETS

PREP TIME: 15 MINUTES • **COOK TIME:** 10 MINUTES

I love spicy food; it's one of the best pleasures in life. When the spice level is just right, there's a perfect balance between heat and flavor that makes the food taste amazing. I believe sriracha has that ideal balance I'm looking for in a hot sauce. This spicy recipe doesn't require you to grind your chicken, which saves you a lot of time and hassle when it comes to making nuggets. It also makes them juicier than your average chicken nuggets. I hope you enjoy!

MAKES 1 SERVING

1 pound (454g) chicken breast

2 large eggs

½ cup breadcrumbs

3 cups frying oil

3 tablespoons sriracha sauce

1 tablespoon honey

SPECIAL EQUIPMENT

Candy/deep-fry thermometer

1. Cut the chicken breast into small cubes.
2. Crack the eggs into a small bowl and beat them. Add the breadcrumbs to a separate small bowl.
3. Add the frying oil to a medium pot and place it over medium heat. Heat the oil to 325°F (160°C), using a deep-fry thermometer to measure the temperature.
4. Toss the chicken cubes in the bowl of beaten eggs and fully coat. Transfer them to the bowl of breadcrumbs and fully coat.
5. Fry the chicken cubes in the oil until golden brown, 3 to 5 minutes. Transfer them to a plate lined with paper towels.
6. In a small pan over medium-low heat, mix the sriracha and honey for 2 minutes, stirring constantly.
7. In a medium bowl, toss the fried chicken nuggets in the sriracha-honey sauce until fully covered. Serve and enjoy!

VARIATION

You can substitute the sriracha for any kind of preferred hot sauce.

FULLY LOADED NACHOS

PREP TIME: 15 MINUTES • **COOK TIME:** 15 MINUTES

As a child, I used to visit a restaurant in Hollywood called Fred62 with my father where I would always order their fully loaded nachos. It was amazing how simple yet delicious the dish was. I wanted to recreate those nachos to capture that nostalgic feeling, and after a few attempts, I nailed the consistency and taste. From the type of meat to the nacho cheese, I figured out the perfect combination to make these nachos a hit.

MAKES 3-4 SERVINGS

- 1 pound (454g) skirt steak
- 1 teaspoon salt
- 2 teaspoons paprika
- 2 tablespoons olive oil
- 2 tablespoons butter
- 2 tablespoons all-purpose flour
- 1 cup milk
- 8 ounces (227g) shredded cheddar cheese
- 5.5 ounces (156g) tortilla chips
- 1 medium tomato, diced
- 1 medium avocado, pitted and diced
- 1 medium fresh jalapeño, stem and ribs removed, sliced
- 2 tablespoons sour cream
- ¼ cup chopped fresh cilantro

1. Dice the skirt steak into small square pieces and season with the salt, paprika, and olive oil, mixing it well to fully coat the meat.
2. Place a medium pan over medium-high heat and stir-fry the steak cubes until they have a slightly charred exterior with a rich brown color and are fully cooked. Remove from the heat and set aside.
3. Prepare the cheese sauce. Place a medium pan over medium-low heat, add the butter and flour, and mix until the butter melts and the flour is well combined with the butter.
4. Add the milk and shredded cheddar cheese. Use additional milk as needed until the sauce comes to your desired thickness. Stir continually while cooking until all is fully melted and combined.
5. On a serving plate, place the tortilla chips and pour the melted cheese over top. Next, add the tomato, avocado, jalapeño, and skirt steak and top with sour cream and chopped cilantro. Enjoy!

PIZZA IN A PAN

PREP TIME: 10 MINUTES • **COOK TIME:** 8 MINUTES

Can you believe this pizza recipe doesn't need an oven at all?! I came up with this recipe when I was camping with some friends, and we craved pizza but had no oven. I started experimenting with what we had, which was a portable stove and a pan. Voilà, the Pizza in a Pan was born. Another great thing about this recipe is that you don't have to wait for the dough to rise; just mix the ingredients together and get started on the pizza right away.

MAKES 1 PAN PIZZA

½ cup all-purpose flour, plus more for work surface

½ teaspoon baking powder

½ teaspoon salt

⅓ cup Greek yogurt

2 tablespoons pizza sauce

4 tablespoons shredded mozzarella cheese

10 pepperoni slices

Fresh basil (optional)

SPECIAL EQUIPMENT

Rolling pin

1. In a medium bowl, combine the flour, baking powder, salt, and Greek yogurt. Mix the ingredients together until a rough dough is formed.

2. Knead the dough for 3 to 4 minutes on a lightly floured work surface until soft.

3. Using a rolling pin, roll the dough into a thin circle matching the size of a medium frying pan.

4. Lightly oil a 10-inch (25cm) nonstick frying pan and place it over medium heat. Add the dough to the pan and cook it until the bottom is golden brown, about 3 to 5 minutes.

5. Flip the dough to the other side and layer the pizza sauce, cheese, and pepperoni over the top. Cover the pan with a lid and let the pizza cook until the cheese melts. Remove from the heat, garnish with fresh basil, slice, and serve.

VARIATION

Feel free to swap the toppings with any you prefer.

KETCHUP CHIPS

PREP TIME: 30 MINUTES • **COOK TIME:** 40 MINUTES

My Canadian friends always told me how delicious ketchup chips were. Unfortunately, you can't easily find ketchup chips in the United States, and I needed to try them for myself. Instead of flying to Canada, I saved a ton of money and made them at home. It's like eating French fries and ketchup but is much more convenient.

MAKES 2-3 SERVINGS
⅓ cup ketchup
2 large russet potatoes
3 cups frying oil
1 teaspoon salt

SPECIAL EQUIPMENT
High-speed blender
Candy/deep-fry thermometer

1. Preheat the oven to 300°F (150°C).
2. On a large baking sheet lined with parchment paper, spread the ketchup into a thin layer and place it in the oven for about 35 minutes until dehydrated and crispy. Remove from the oven and let cool.
3. Break up the dehydrated ketchup into small pieces and transfer them to a high-speed blender. Blend on high until powdered.
4. Peel and thinly slice the potatoes, then soak the slices in ice cold water for 5 minutes to remove the starch. Remove the potatoes from the water and pat the potato slices with paper towels until fully dry.
5. Add the frying oil to a medium pot and place it over medium heat. Bring the oil to 350°F (180°C), using a deep-fry thermometer to measure the temperature.
6. Fry the potatoes until golden brown and crispy, 3 to 5 minutes.
7. Transfer the potato chips to a medium bowl and toss with the ketchup powder and salt.

CHEESE DONUTS

PREP TIME: 15 MINUTES, PLUS 45 MINUTES TO FREEZE • **COOK TIME:** 15 MINUTES

Listen, donuts are amazing—they're probably one of my favorite desserts. But what if we removed the sugar, the glaze, and the dough, and replaced them with cheese? The results are pretty amazing. You get a gooey, cheesy texture that you'll endlessly want to devour!

MAKES 6 DONUTS

One 16-ounce (454g) block low-moisture mozzarella cheese

One 8-ounce (227g) bag Crunchy Cheetos (see Note)

1½ cups all-purpose flour

2 large eggs

4 cups frying oil

SPECIAL EQUIPMENT

Donut mold

Rolling pin

Candy/deep-fry thermometer

1. Fit a small pot with a medium nonreactive metal or heatproof glass bowl; the bowl shouldn't touch the bottom of the pot but should sit in the top half of the pot. Set the bowl aside.

2. Place the small pot filled halfway with water over medium heat and bring to a boil.

3. Meanwhile, cut the mozzarella block into small cubes, about ½ inch (1.25cm) each.

4. Add the cheese cubes to the medium heatproof bowl. Place the bowl over the pot of boiling water, ensuring the bowl doesn't cause the water to overflow. (Discard a little water if needed.) Stir the cheese until it's fully melted.

5. Pour the melted cheese into a standard 6-piece donut mold.

6. Place the mold in the freezer for at least 45 minutes until the cheese hardens.

7. Using a rolling pin, smash the Cheetos in the bag until well crushed. To avoid chips exploding all over your counter, carefully open the bag a little at the top to release any air.

8. Prepare three small bowls. Place the flour in one bowl, crack the eggs into another bowl and then beat them, and pour the crushed Cheetos into the third bowl.

9. Once the cheese donuts have hardened, remove the mold from the freezer and remove one donut from the mold. First, toss the donut in the flour, then dip into the beaten eggs, and finally toss in the crushed Cheetos, ensuring it's fully coated at each step. Place the battered ring on a plate or wire rack and repeat the process with the remaining donuts.

10. Add the frying oil to a large pot and place it over medium heat. Bring the oil to 350°F (180°C), using a deep-fry thermometer to measure the temperature.

11. Working in batches, fry the donuts in the hot oil for 2 to 5 minutes, until crispy. Using a slotted spoon, transfer the cheese donuts from the oil to a dish lined with paper towels and serve immediately.

NOTE

If you're not a fan of Cheetos, many other crunchy snacks make great substitutes for Cheetos in this recipe.

SCALLOPED POTATOES

PREP TIME: 20 MINUTES • **COOK TIME:** 1 HOUR

There are not many things in my life that make me as happy as potatoes. They're versatile, delicious, and can be transformed into so many comforting and satisfying dishes, like this one. It's the perfect side dish for any hearty meal, and it's easy to make, impressing your friends and family. This dish can make even a novice cook feel like Gordon Ramsay!

MAKES A 9×13-INCH PAN

3 pounds (1.4kg) Yukon Gold potatoes

1½ teaspoons salt, divided

6 tablespoons cold butter, diced and divided

1 cup milk

4 tablespoons all-purpose flour

½ cup shredded cheddar cheese

1 tablespoon chopped fresh parsley

1. Preheat the oven to 425°F (220°C).
2. Peel the potatoes and cut them into ¼-inch (6mm) slices.
3. In a 9×13-inch (23×33cm) baking dish, add a layer of potato slices until the bottom is covered, sprinkle ½ teaspoon salt over the potatoes and scatter 2 tablespoons diced butter over the layer. Repeat the process two more times until you have 3 layers of potatoes.
4. Mix the milk and flour together and pour the milk mixture into the baking dish.
5. Bake for 15 minutes, then remove the potatoes from the oven and cover the top with the shredded cheddar cheese. Reduce the oven temperature to 375°F (190°C) and place the baking dish back in the oven to cook for 45 minutes or until richly brown in color.
6. Remove the dish from the oven, sprinkle parsley over the top, and serve.

VARIATION
Any type of potatoes will work in this recipe.

POTATO CHEESE STICKS

PREP TIME: 15 MINUTES, PLUS 30 MINUTES FREEZE TIME • **COOK TIME:** 30 MINUTES

Stop what you're doing right now and run to the kitchen! I'm too excited for you to try this recipe. It's like having French fries from the future. (Just hear me out on this one.) The combination of these ingredients creates a super-crispy potato cheese stick with a creamy, soft inside. If there's anything you should 100 percent try in this entire cookbook, it's this recipe. You will instantly fall in love.

MAKES 1 SERVING

2 large russet potatoes
½ cup cornstarch
1 cup shredded mozzarella cheese
1 teaspoon salt
3 cups frying oil

SPECIAL EQUIPMENT

Potato masher
Rolling pin
Candy/deep-fry thermometer

1. Peel and roughly chop the potatoes.
2. Bring a medium pot of water to a boil over medium heat and then boil the chopped potatoes until very soft, about 15 minutes.
3. Drain the potatoes and transfer them to a large bowl. Mash them using a potato masher or fork until smooth.
4. In the same bowl, add the cornstarch, mozzarella cheese, and salt and mix well until it has a doughlike consistency. Knead it with your hands for about 1 minute until pliable.
5. Transfer the mashed potato mixture into a medium sealable plastic bag and flatten it using a rolling pin. Place the flattened bag in the freezer for 30 minutes.
6. Meanwhile, add the frying oil to a medium pot and place it over medium heat. Bring the oil to 350°F (180°C), using a deep-fry thermometer to measure the temperature.
7. Remove the bag from the freezer and remove the flattened potatoes from the bag. Cut the frozen potato mixture into French fry shapes and place them on a plate or baking sheet lined with parchment paper.
8. Working in small batches to prevent the fries from sticking together, fry the potato sticks in the hot oil until golden brown and crispy, 5 to 8 minutes each batch.
9. Transfer the Potato Cheese Sticks to a plate lined with paper towels to cool slightly before serving.

MAINS, SIDES & BREADS

TENDER BEEF SHORT RIBS

PREP TIME: 10 MINUTES • **COOK TIME:** 4 HOURS

These beef short ribs are among the most tender meats you'll ever cook! The hours of oven time help break down the collagen and connective tissues in the meat, leaving you with the best results. Pair these ribs with your favorite side dish like steamed rice or mashed potatoes and enjoy!

MAKES 5-6 SERVINGS

- 4-6 pounds (1.8-2.7kg) short ribs, separated
- Salt, to taste
- Pepper, to taste
- 1 large white onion, roughly chopped
- 2 tablespoons tomato paste
- 1½ cups red wine (see Note)
- 4 cups beef or chicken broth
- 2 pods whole star anise
- 3 garlic cloves, minced

1. Season the short ribs with salt and pepper.
2. In a large Dutch oven (or another large ovensafe pot with a lid) placed over high heat, sear all sides of the short ribs until they brown and a crust forms, 5 or 6 minutes. Remove the short ribs and set them aside.
3. Preheat the oven to 300°F (150°C).
4. In the same Dutch oven, add the onions and cook them in the rib juices until slightly brown.
5. Add the tomato paste, red wine, broth, star anise, and minced garlic.
6. Place the short ribs back into the Dutch oven, cover with the lid, and place in the oven to cook for 3 hours, stirring once halfway through.
7. Carefully remove the Dutch oven from the oven and transfer the ribs to a plate, reserving the broth.
8. Transfer 1 cup of broth from the Dutch oven into a medium pan over medium-low heat. Discard any solids.
9. Cook the broth until it reduces to ⅓ cup, 5 to 8 minutes, then pour it over the ribs and serve.

NOTE

I recommend using the cheapest red wine you can find for this recipe. You're going to cook off the alcohol, so the price or quality of the wine won't matter much.

STREET TACOS

PREP TIME: 15 MINUTES, PLUS 30 MINUTES TO MARINATE • **COOK TIME:** 20 MINUTES

When you grow up in Los Angeles, you eat a lot of tacos. After a long night of partying or just a long night at work, my friends and I always hit up taco trucks for a cheap, delicious, and satisfying meal. Every taco truck owner has their own unique style of marinating the meat. I gathered tips from the best to create this recipe, which features a simple rub made with paprika, salt, and pepper.

MAKES 4 SERVINGS

- 1 pound (454g) flank steak or skirt steak, cut into bite-size cubes
- 2 tablespoon olive oil, divided
- 2 tablespoons paprika
- 1 teaspoon salt
- 1 teaspoon pepper
- ½ large white onion, finely diced
- 1 bunch fresh cilantro, finely chopped
- 6 flour or corn tortillas (see Note)
- Sauces or toppings of choice
- Juice of 1 lime

1. Coat the steak with 1 tablespoon olive oil and the paprika, salt, and pepper. Place it in the fridge for about 30 minutes to marinate.
2. Lightly grease a large skillet with the remaining 1 tablespoon olive oil and place it over high heat. Cook the steak in the skillet until a slight crust develops, 15 to 20 minutes.
3. Build the tacos by placing the desired amount of steak, onion, and cilantro on each tortilla, followed by any preferred sauces or other toppings you enjoy. Squeeze some lime juice over the top and enjoy.

NOTE

I like to warm the tortillas up by wrapping them in a paper towel and microwaving them for about 30 seconds each. You can also heat them up in a pan with some oil.

VARIATION

Consider swapping out the steak for other proteins, such as chicken or ground beef, if preferred.

HONEY-BUTTER FRIED CHICKEN

PREP TIME: 15 MINUTES • **COOK TIME:** 30 MINUTES

Get ready to taste the best fried chicken of your life. The sweet and salty flavors of this Honey Butter Fried Chicken are absolutely amazing. It's also one of the crispiest pieces of fried chicken you will ever have, thanks to the secret ingredient: ice-cold water. This is what takes battered chicken to the next level!

MAKES 3-4 SERVINGS

1 pound (454g) boneless, skinless chicken thighs
½ cup all-purpose flour
½ cup cornstarch
½ teaspoon baking soda
½ cup ice-cold water
2 cups frying oil
½ stick butter
2 tablespoons honey
2 tablespoons soy sauce

SPECIAL EQUIPMENT
Candy/deep-fry thermometer

1. Cut the chicken into 1½-inch (3.8cm) slices and place them in a medium bowl.
2. Add the flour, cornstarch, baking soda, and ice-cold water and mix until well combined and the chicken slices are fully coated.
3. Pour the frying oil into a medium pot over medium heat. Heat the oil to 350°F (180°C), using a deep-fry thermometer to measure the temperature
4. Working in batches, fry the coated chicken slices in the hot oil until golden brown, 8 to 10 minutes. Transfer the fried chicken to a plate lined with paper towels.
5. To make the sauce, place the butter, honey, and soy sauce in a large saucepan over medium heat and stir well until heated through, 4 to 5 minutes.
6. Once the sauce is ready, add the fried chicken to the saucepan and mix well until the chicken is fully coated in the sauce.

VARIATION
Chicken breasts or wings also work well in this recipe.

ORANGE CHICKEN

PREP TIME: 5 MINUTES • **COOK TIME:** 20 MINUTES

Orange Chicken has to be my favorite menu item at Panda Express. I wanted to make some at home, but when I looked up a recipe, the ingredients list was longer than a grocery store receipt, so I made this shortcut recipe that tastes just as good. Is it traditional? No. But in reality, there is no "traditional," since orange chicken is an American invention. Skip the difficult route and save time with this recipe!

MAKES 1 SERVING

10 ounces (283g) frozen chicken nuggets

2 tablespoons barbecue sauce

¼ cup orange marmalade

1 tablespoons soy sauce

1. Heat up the chicken nuggets according to the package instructions.
2. To make the sauce, add the barbecue sauce, orange marmalade, and soy sauce to a medium skillet over medium-low heat. Cook, stirring continuously, for 2 to 5 minutes.
3. Toss the chicken nuggets in the sauce until fully coated.

CHEESE-STUFFED BREAD

PREP TIME: 30 MINUTES, PLUS 1 HOUR TO RISE • **COOK TIME:** 35 MINUTES

I can safely say that almost everyone loves cheese and bread. It's the perfect combination, no matter what types you use. This recipe takes that idea to the next level by stuffing the bread with cheese before baking it in the oven. Bread making can be challenging for beginners, but I've ensured this recipe is foolproof and has a 0 percent failure rate.

MAKES 1 LOAF

- 1⅓ cups all-purpose flour, plus more for work surface
- 1 teaspoon active dry yeast
- ⅓ cup milk
- 5 tablespoons melted butter, plus more for garnish
- ½ teaspoon salt
- 1 cup shredded mozzarella cheese
- Chopped fresh parsley, for garnish

1. In a medium bowl, mix the flour, yeast, milk, melted butter, and salt until a dough forms.

2. On a lightly floured work surface, knead the dough for 5 to 10 minutes until softened. Form the dough into a ball and place it in a large bowl. Cover the bowl with a clean dish towel and let the dough rest at room temperature for at least 1 hour or until it doubles in size.

3. Meanwhile, preheat the oven to 325°F (165°C). Line a baking sheet with parchment paper and set aside.

4. Once the dough has doubled in size, remove it from the bowl, cut it in half, and stretch each piece until it is 8 to 10 inches (20 to 25cm) in length.

5. Place the shredded mozzarella cheese down the center of one piece of dough and then cover it with the other piece, pinching the edges of the dough to seal the cheese inside and tucking the edges underneath.

6. Place the dough on the prepared baking sheet and bake for 35 minutes, until golden brown.

7. Remove the bread from the oven, brush the top with additional melted butter, and garnish with parsley before serving immediately.

BUBBLE SHRIMP

PREP TIME: 10 MINUTES • **COOK TIME:** 4 MINUTES

I've always been a fan of fried shrimp. I usually make a batter, dip my shrimp, and fry them up, but one day I experimented by adding baking powder to the batter and POOF, it bubbled! It's such a fun approach to fried shrimp, and it gives them a new sort of mouthfeel with the space between the batter and shrimp.

MAKES 5 PIECES

- 1 pound (454g) jumbo shrimp, with tails on, peeled and deveined
- ½ teaspoon salt
- ½ teaspoon pepper
- ⅔ cup cornstarch
- 2 tablespoons all-purpose flour
- 4 tablespoons water
- 1 teaspoon baking powder
- 2½ cups frying oil, divided
- 3 egg whites
- Flaky sea salt, to taste

SPECIAL EQUIPMENT

Candy/deep-fry thermometer

1. Place the shrimp in a small bowl and season with the salt and pepper. Set aside.
2. In a medium bowl, mix the cornstarch, flour, water, baking powder, ½ cup frying oil, and egg whites. Whisk until fully combined.
3. Dip the shrimp into the mixture until fully coated.
4. In a medium pot over medium heat, add the remaining 2 cups frying oil. Heat the oil to 350°F (180°C), using a deep-fry thermometer to measure the temperature.
5. Fry the shrimp until it bubbles and turns golden brown on both sides, 2 to 4 minutes (see Note). Sprinkle with flaky sea salt and serve.

NOTE

If the shrimp isn't bubbling easily, add a little more baking powder to the batter mixture.

LULE KABOBS

PREP TIME: 15 MINUTES • **COOK TIME:** 15 MINUTES

This recipe is dedicated to my father. The images you see here are the last ones taken of him before he passed away. I feel incredibly lucky to have shared this moment with him before his cancer worsened, and I'm grateful to be able to honor him in this cookbook. My father perfected this recipe for lule kabobs. It was the first dish he taught me how to make, and it was our favorite. He was always in the kitchen cooking up amazing meals, and this one was our favorite. There are a ton of different kinds of lule kabob recipes out there, but my dad always said, "Keeping it simple will allow the flavors of the meat to shine through." And that's exactly what I have done.

MAKES 3 SKEWERS

1 pound (454g) ground beef
1 teaspoon salt
1 teaspoon pepper
1 medium white onion
1 cup cooked rice (optional)
2 grilled tomatoes (optional)

SPECIAL EQUIPMENT

Cheesecloth
Skewers (if using bamboo skewers, soak them before using)
Food processor

1. Season the ground beef with the salt and pepper and then set aside.

2. Roughly chop the onion into chunks and put them in a food processor to mince or create a purée. Place the onion in the middle of a cheesecloth and squeeze out the excess water from the onion.

3. In a medium bowl, combine the ground beef and onion, mixing them together well.

4. Preheat a gas grill to high heat or start a charcoal grill.

5. Slightly wet your hands, then scoop one third of the meat mixture and mold it onto a skewer, shaping it into a long sausage-like shape. Press the meat firmly onto the skewer to ensure it holds together. Place the skewer on a plate and repeat with the remaining two skewers.

6. Cook the kabobs on the hot grill for 4 to 6 minutes per side or until cooked through and nicely browned on the outside.

7. Serve the kabobs immediately with rice and grilled tomatoes, if using, or your favorite accompaniments.

LEMON-PEPPER WINGS

PREP TIME: 15 MINUTES • **COOK TIME:** 24 MINUTES

Lemon-pepper wings are the next best thing to hot wings. You get this zesty flavor with a peppery kick that's unbelievably delicious. Every time I go to my favorite wing shop, I order half hot wings and half lemon-pepper wings. I'm glad someone figured out this delicious pairing because I don't want to know what life would be like without them.

MAKES 3 SERVINGS

- 3 pounds (1.4kg) segmented chicken wings
- 2 tablespoons cornstarch
- 1 tablespoon olive oil
- 1 teaspoon garlic powder
- 1 teaspoon onion powder
- 1 teaspoon paprika
- 3 teaspoons lemon-pepper seasoning, divided
- 4 cups frying oil
- ¾ cup unsalted butter
- Juice of 1 lemon
- 1 tablespoon honey

SPECIAL EQUIPMENT

Candy/deep-fry thermometer

1. In a large bowl, add the chicken wings, cornstarch, olive oil, garlic powder, onion powder, paprika, and teaspoon lemon-pepper seasoning and mix everything together until all the wings are fully coated.

2. To a large pot over medium heat, add the vegetable oil. Heat the oil to 375°F (190°C), using a deep-fry thermometer to measure the temperature.

3. In two batches, place the chicken wings into the hot oil and fry them until golden brown, 10 to 12 minutes. Remove from the oil and place on a plate lined with paper towels to drain.

4. Prepare the lemon-pepper sauce. In a medium pot over medium heat, add the butter, lemon juice, remaining 2 teaspoons lemon-pepper seasoning, and honey. Melt the butter and continuously stir the sauce for 3 to 5 minutes until well mixed and heated through.

5. Add the cooked wings to a large bowl. Pour the lemon-pepper sauce over the wings, toss until fully coated, and serve.

NOTE

For segmented chicken wings, buy precut wings, drumettes, or party wings.

MAC & CHEESE

PREP TIME: 5 MINUTES • **COOK TIME:** 20 MINUTES

Making mac and cheese shouldn't be a strenuous process. Most recipes require 10+ ingredients, which always deters me from making them. I don't want to spend all my time in the kitchen making mac and cheese, so I developed this few-ingredient mac and cheese recipe that tastes as delicious as any other.

MAKES 4 SERVINGS

4½ cups milk

12 ounces (340g) uncooked macaroni pasta

½ teaspoon salt

7 ounces (198g) shredded cheddar cheese

3 tablespoons butter

1. In a large pot over medium heat, add the milk and bring it to a slight boil, stirring occasionally to prevent burning.

2. Add the macaroni and salt to the pot and cook for about 15 minutes, until all the milk is absorbed by the pasta. If you have milk remaining, just leave it in the pot.

3. Once the pasta is cooked and the milk is mostly absorbed, add the cheese and butter to the pot, then mix until the cheese is fully melted and combined.

VARIATION

You can swap out the dairy milk for a substitute, if desired. I suggest a creamy cashew or oat milk. Make sure to add salt to taste when using nut milks.

PAN BREAD

PREP TIME: 10 MINUTES, PLUS 1 HOUR AND 15 MINUTES TO RISE • **COOK TIME:** 20 MINUTES

You might not realize it, but many recipes typically made in the oven can also be made in a pan on the stove. Of course, temperatures and processes change a bit, but it's not impossible. This pan bread recipe can be made if you're outdoors or if you don't have an oven. It tastes as good as any regular bread made in the oven, and it has the soft, chewy texture you only get from homemade bread.

MAKES 6 SERVINGS

- 2 cups all-purpose flour, plus more for work surface
- ¾ cup whole milk
- 1 tablespoon olive oil
- 2 teaspoons instant yeast
- ½ teaspoon salt
- 1 tablespoon sesame seeds (optional)

1. In a large bowl, add the flour, milk, olive oil, yeast, and salt and mix well until a dough forms.
2. Lightly flour a work surface and knead the dough on it for 5 to 7 minutes until smooth and elastic. Place the kneaded dough back in the bowl.
3. Cover the bowl with a clean kitchen towel and let it sit at room temperature to rise for at least 1 hour.
4. Into a lightly oiled 10-inch (25cm) frying pan, place the dough and stretch it out. Sprinkle sesame seeds over the dough, if using. Cover the pan with a lid and let it sit for 15 minutes more.
5. Place the pan over low heat and cook the dough for about 10 minutes with the lid on.
6. Flip the bread, replace the cover, and cook the bread for about 10 minutes on the other side. Once golden brown on both sides, serve.

FALL-OFF-THE-BONE BARBECUE RIBS

PREP TIME: 10 MINUTES • **COOK TIME:** 2 HOURS AND 6 MINUTES

I used to think I needed a giant smoker or grill to make prefect ribs at home, but I never had those because I've always lived in small apartments. So I developed this recipe that only requires an oven, yet it doesn't lack the smokiness, flavor, or texture we all love. These ribs are fall-off-the-bone tender, and you don't need any giant outdoor equipment to make them!

MAKES 4 SERVINGS

2 pounds (907g) pork baby back ribs
Juice of 1 lemon
1 teaspoon pepper
½ teaspoon garlic powder
½ teaspoon onion powder
1 teaspoon salt
2 teaspoons chili powder
1 teaspoon mustard powder
2 teaspoons paprika
¼ cup brown sugar
½ cup barbecue sauce

1. Cut up the rack of ribs into individual rib pieces.
2. Coat the ribs in the lemon juice, rubbing it in well.
3. In a small bowl, combine the pepper, garlic powder, onion powder, salt, chili powder, mustard powder, paprika, and brown sugar.
4. Rub the seasoning mix all over the ribs, coating them well.
5. Preheat the oven to 300°F (150°C).
6. Place the ribs onto a baking sheet and then tightly cover it with aluminum foil.
7. Bake the ribs for 2 hours.
8. Remove the baking sheet from the oven, take off the foil and discard it, and drain the fat into a small heatproof glass or metal bowl to let cool before discarding the fat. Brush the ribs with barbecue sauce.
9. Return the baking sheet to the oven and broil the ribs for 2 to 3 additional minutes on each side before serving (see Note).

NOTE

You may need to adjust the final cook time in step 9, depending on the distance between the ribs and the broiler. The sauce should look slightly bubbly and dark amber in color—then you can take the ribs out of the broiler.

CHEESE-STUFFED FLATBREADS

PREP TIME: 10 MINUTES, PLUS 1 HOUR TO RISE • **COOK TIME:** 30-35 MINUTES

You can never go wrong with cheese and bread—it's the perfect combination that just works so well. Making bread can be intimidating if you don't know what the texture of the dough should feel like or how to tell if it's fully baked. There's a lot of room for error. Not with this recipe—it's super easy to make, and I guarantee you can't mess it up! I've perfected this recipe so even a novice cook can make it. The best part is, you don't need an oven.

MAKES 6 FLATBREADS

½ cup milk

½ cup water

1 teaspoon instant yeast

1¾ cups all-purpose flour, plus more for work surface

1 teaspoon salt

1 tablespoon olive oil, plus more for garnish

1 cup shredded mozzarella cheese

2 tablespoons chopped fresh parsley, for garnish

SPECIAL EQUIPMENT

Rolling pin

1. In a medium bowl, add the milk, water, yeast, flour, and salt and mix until well combined. Then add the olive oil and mix again.

2. On a lightly floured work surface, knead the dough for 10 minutes, shape it into a ball, place in a large bowl, and cover the bowl with a clean dish towel. Let the dough sit at room temperature for at least 1 hour to rise. If the dough feels too wet, add more flour until you get a slightly sticky consistency.

3. Cut the dough into 6 equal pieces, roll each into a ball, and press down in the middle of each with your thumb to create a crevasse.

4. Stuff each crevasse with an equal portion of shredded mozzarella, then roll it into a ball and place it on a baking sheet.

5. Using a rolling pin, flatten each dough ball until it's about 7 inches (18cm) in diameter and place on a baking sheet.

6. Heat a medium frying pan over medium heat. One at a time, cook each piece of flattened dough until browned and then flip it and brown the other side, about 3 minutes on each side.

7. Brush each flatbread with additional olive oil and garnish with an equal portion of parsley. Serve.

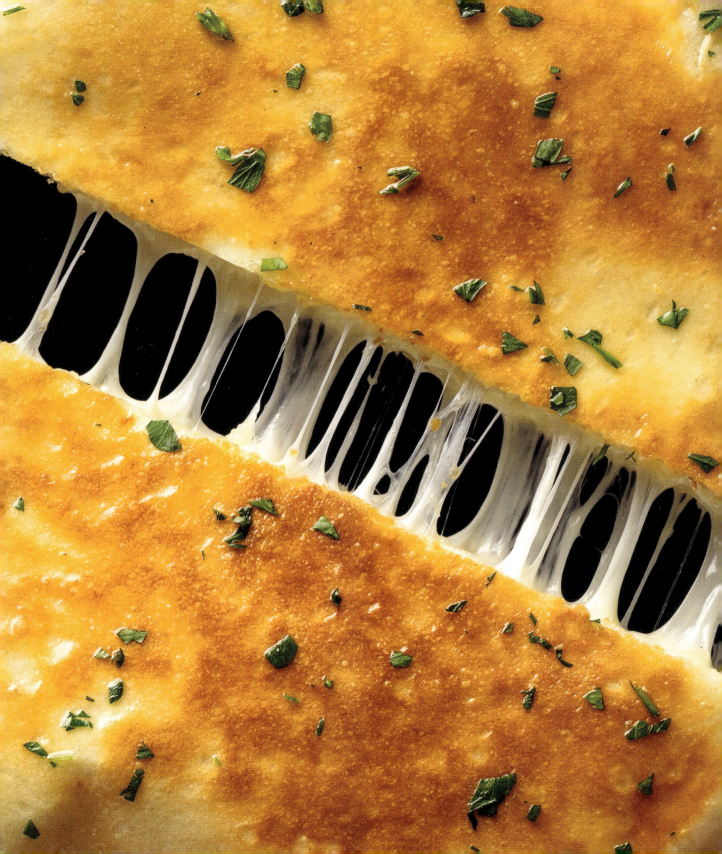

3-INGREDIENT FLOUR TORTILLAS

PREP TIME: 20 MINUTES, PLUS 20 MINUTES TO REST • **COOK TIME:** 48 MINUTES

This flour tortilla recipe is a new approach to making tortillas. Traditionally, they are made with lard or vegetable shortening, but I replaced these with heavy cream. This gives the tortillas a smooth texture and a somewhat creamy flavor, resulting in an amazing taste. Use these tortillas to make tacos or even burritos—you will absolutely love them!

MAKES 12 TORTILLAS

4 cups all-purpose flour, plus more for work surface

1 teaspoon salt

2½ cups heavy cream

SPECIAL EQUIPMENT

Rolling pin

1. Mix all the ingredients together in a large bowl until a dough forms.
2. Prepare a work surface with a dusting of flour. Knead the dough on the floured surface for 15 to 20 minutes until it becomes soft.
3. Cut the dough in 12 pieces of equal size and roll each piece into a small ball.
4. Cover the dough balls with a clean dish towel and let them sit for 20 minutes.
5. Using a rolling pin, roll out each dough ball to about 10 inches (25cm) across.
6. In a medium frying pan over medium heat, cook each tortilla for about 2 minutes on each side or until it's lightly brown.

SMASH BURGER

PREP TIME: 30 MINUTES • **COOK TIME:** 45 MINUTES

A burger has to be one of my all-time favorite dishes on the planet. It's the perfect sandwich, balancing protein, vegetables, and carbs. I do modify my burger a bit—I'm a true believer that lettuce doesn't belong on a burger. I also believe that a burger should be simple, with just a few ingredients that complement the meat and don't compete with it. This smash burger achieves the perfect balance and is a must-try.

MAKES 2 BURGERS

1 tablespoon vegetable oil
1 medium white onion, thinly sliced
1 pound (454g) ground beef
1 teaspoon salt
1 teaspoon black pepper
2 slices cheese of choice
1 tablespoon butter
2 burger buns
1 tomato, sliced
Sauce of choice

1. In a medium pan over low heat, add the oil and the sliced onions. Cook until they caramelize, about 35 minutes.

2. Shape the ground beef into four 4-ounce (113g) balls, then season them with salt and pepper.

3. Place a large pan over medium heat, once it's hot, add the ground beef balls and press them down with a burger press or a large spatula until completely flat.

4. Cook one side of the patties until a nice crust forms, about 5 minutes, then flip the patties and add sliced cheese on top of two. Cover the pan and let the cheese fully melt and then remove from the heat.

5. Spread the butter on the buns. In a medium pan placed over medium-low heat, toast the buns buttered-side down until light brown in color.

6. Assemble the burgers with the toasted buns, burger patties (one plain and one with cheese for each burger), caramelized onions, tomato slices, and your favorite sauce.

SPICY PEANUT NOODLES

PREP TIME: 10 MINUTES • **COOK TIME:** 20 MINUTES

Anything with peanut butter in it has my name all over it. My favorite candy is Reese's Peanut Butter Cups, and it's not because of the chocolate. Peanut butter is often used in sweet desserts or candy, but I wanted to try it in a savory dish—and I'm so glad I did, because these spicy peanut noodles are by far my favorite noodles ever.

MAKES 1 BOWL

3 tablespoons peanut butter

2 teaspoons soy sauce

2 teaspoons rice wine vinegar

½ teaspoon sesame oil

2 tablespoons chili crisp

1 tablespoon minced fresh ginger

1 garlic clove, minced

3 tablespoons water

One 7-ounce (198g) package udon noodles

Toasted sesame seeds, for serving (optional)

Fresh scallions, chopped, for serving (optional)

1. In a medium pot, combine the peanut butter, soy sauce, rice wine vinegar, sesame oil, chili crisp, minced ginger, and minced garlic.

2. Place the pot over medium heat and stir while heating until well combined. Add the water to thin the sauce out a bit.

3. In a separate medium pot, cook the noodles according to the package directions.

4. Drain the cooked noodles, add them to the pot of peanut sauce, and mix until the noodles are fully covered in the sauce. If the mixture is too thick, add some pasta water to thin it out.

5. Transfer the noodles to a serving bowl and garnish with toasted sesame seeds and scallions, if using.

VARIATION

Many types of packaged noodles work for this recipe. Feel free to use whatever kind you prefer.

LOLLIPOP BARBECUE WINGS

PREP TIME: 20 MINUTES • **COOK TIME:** 8 MINUTES

This new approach to barbecue wings is perfect for any occasion. Giving the drumstick a lollipop shape makes for a clean eating experience, which usually isn't the case with wings. It's aesthetically appealing and surprisingly easy to achieve. You'll have lots of fun with this one!

MAKES 6 WINGS
6 chicken drumsticks
½ cup all-purpose flour
½ cup cornstarch
1 teaspoon salt
2 large eggs
3 cups frying oil
1 cup barbecue sauce

SPECIAL EQUIPMENT
Candy/deep-fry thermometer

1. Cut a slit in the middle of the drumstick horizontally to the bone, remove the meat from the cut to the end with the least amount of meat to fully expose the bone. Then push up the remaining meat on the other half to create a round shape on top of the drumstick. Repeat for all remaining drumsticks. Discard the removed meat and skin. Set the lollipop-shaped drumsticks aside.

2. In a medium bowl, mix together the flour, cornstarch, and salt.

3. In a small bowl, beat the eggs.

4. Dip the drumsticks in the beaten eggs and then in the dry mixture. Repeat the process twice for each drumstick.

5. Add the frying oil to a large saucepan and place it over medium heat. Bring the oil to 350°F (180°C), using a deep-fry thermometer to measure the temperature.

6. Fry the drumsticks in the hot oil until golden brown, 5 to 8 minutes. Transfer the wings to a wire rack or plate lined with paper towels to drain the excess oil.

7. Dip the drumsticks in your favorite barbecue sauce and serve.

HOT WINGS

PREP TIME: 10 MINUTES • **COOK TIME:** 1 HOUR

I used to work at Domino's Pizza, and we would always get free food. The one thing I loved making was hot wings, but I wouldn't make them the way Domino's wanted us to. I would change up the process and the hot sauce to get the maximum amount of flavor. After leaving Domino's, I ended up making this recipe weekly for years because of how delicious it is. Just make sure not to skip any steps and enjoy your new favorite wings!

MAKES 16 WINGS

- 16 segmented chicken wings (see Note)
- 2 teaspoons baking powder
- 2 teaspoons garlic powder
- 1½ teaspoons salt
- 1 teaspoon black pepper
- ¼ cup hot sauce of choice
- 4 tablespoons unsalted butter
- 2 tablespoons honey

1. Preheat the oven to 400°F (200°C).
2. In a large bowl, add the chicken wings, baking powder, garlic powder, salt, and pepper. Mix well until every wing is evenly coated with the seasoning.
3. Place the wings on a baking sheet lined with parchment paper. Bake the chicken wings in the oven until golden brown, about 1 hour.
4. Meanwhile, prepare the hot sauce. In a small pot over medium-low heat, add the hot sauce, unsalted butter, and honey. Stir until the butter melts and the ingredients are well combined. Turn off the heat.
5. Remove the wings from the oven, and place the cooked wings in a large bowl and then pour the hot sauce mixture all over the wings. Give them a good toss until the wings are fully coated.

NOTE
For segmented chicken wings, buy precut wings, drumettes, or party wings.

GARLIC NOODLES

PREP TIME: 15 MINUTES • **COOK TIME:** 20 MINUTES

Where are my garlic lovers at? This dish perfectly satisfies those garlic cravings. Many other garlic noodle recipes tend to overpower the other flavors with too much garlic. I made sure this recipe wouldn't be overwhelming but would still deliver the perfect amount of garlic taste, with each ingredient complementing the others.

MAKES 1 SERVING

- 1 tablespoon soy sauce
- 1 tablespoon oyster sauce
- 1 teaspoon fish sauce
- 1 teaspoon granulated sugar
- ¼ teaspoon sesame oil
- 3 tablespoons butter
- 4 garlic cloves, minced
- One 7-ounce (198g) package udon noodles
- 4 tablespoons shredded Parmesan cheese
- Scallions, for garnish (optional)
- Toasted sesame seeds, for garnish (optional)

1. In a small bowl, mix together the soy sauce, oyster sauce, fish sauce, sugar, and sesame oil and set aside.

2. In a medium pan over low heat, melt the butter, then add in the minced garlic and cook for 1 to 2 minutes. Add the soy sauce mixture to the pan, stir well, and remove the pan from the heat. Set aside.

3. In a medium pot, cook the noodles according to the package directions and then drain the water.

4. Place the cooked and drained noodles in the pan with the garlic sauce and mix well until the noodles are well coated.

5. Add the Parmesan cheese to the noodles and toss until fully combined.

6. Garnish with scallions and toasted sesame seeds, if using.

VARIATION

Many types of packaged noodles work for this recipe. Feel free to use whatever kind you prefer.

FALL-OFF-THE-BONE BEEF RIBS

PREP TIME: 5 MINUTES • **COOK TIME:** 3 HOURS AND 35 MINUTES

Pork ribs are a popular restaurant choice, but beef ribs are just as mouthwatering and have a uniquely rich flavor. They're also larger in size and provide an absolutely delicious option for those who can't eat pork. As you'll notice, I've simplified the cooking process as much as possible without sacrificing flavor, and you won't need any special equipment!

MAKES 4 SERVINGS

- 4 pounds (1.8kg) beef ribs
- 2 tablespoons prepared mustard
- 3 tablespoons meat rub (see Note)
- 2 teaspoons salt

1. Preheat the oven to 300°F (150°C).
2. Rub the rib slab with the mustard, coating all sides.
3. Season the ribs with the meat rub and salt, coating well (see Note).
4. Wrap the ribs with aluminum foil, place them in a 12x16-inch (30x40cm) baking pan, and bake for 3 hours and 30 minutes.
5. Remove the baking pan from the oven, remove the foil from one corner, and drain the fat into a small heatproof glass or metal bowl to let cool before discarding it. Remove the aluminum foil from the ribs.
6. Return the baking pan to the oven. Change the oven setting to broil. Cook under the broiler for 5 minutes or until a dark brown crust forms before removing and serving. You may need to adjust the broiling time depending on the distance between the ribs and the broiler.

NOTE

I prefer Kinder's All-Purpose Meat and Veggie Rub for this recipe. You might need to use more meat rub than specified in this recipe, depending on the size of your ribs. Just use as much as it takes to cover them entirely.

CHICHARRONES

PREP TIME: 30 MINUTES • **COOK TIME:** 1 HOUR AND 15 MINUTES

I'll never forget the day I first tried chicharrones. I was in middle school, and my friends wanted to introduce me to this amazing dish, so they took me to a local Mexican restaurant to have me try it. It was so delicious that I went back every week after school just to get a taste of that mouthwatering treat. When I started making it at home, I was shocked at how easy it was to make, and it tasted even better homemade. If you're a fan of bacon or any pork dish, chicharrones will blow you away. The crispy and juicy pork will have you making this dish more often than you probably should, but I won't tell anyone.

MAKES 4-5 SERVINGS

3 pounds (1.4kg) sliced pork belly

1 large white onion, quartered

1 teaspoon salt

2 cups frying oil

Salt, to taste

SPECIAL EQUIPMENT

Candy/deep-fry thermometer

1. Cut the pork belly into 2½-inch (6.25cm) strips.

2. In a large pot, add the cubed pork belly, onion quarters, salt, and enough water to cover the ingredients, about 4 cups.

3. Place the pot over medium heat and bring to a boil. Once boiling, reduce the heat to medium-low and let the pork cook at a simmer, uncovered, for about 45 minutes or until the pork is fully cooked and tender.

4. Transfer the pork to a wire rack and let the water drain until the pork is fully dried. Discard the remaining contents of the pot.

5. Add the frying oil to a large pot and place it over medium heat. Bring the oil to 300°F (150°C), using a deep-fry thermometer to measure the temperature.

6. Fry the pork cubes in the oil for about 20 minutes until lightly brown.

7. Remove the pork cubes from the oil, placing them on a plate lined with paper towels, and then increase the heat to high until the oil reaches 350°F (180°C).

8. Return the pork belley to the pot and fry until richly brown in color, about 10 minutes.

9. Transfer the pork belly back to the plate lined with paper towels to cool for 5 to 10 minutes before salting to taste and serving.

NOTE

Consider serving this recipe with a side of guacamole dip for an amazing combination of flavors.

CAKES, PIES & SWEET BREADS

CAKE POPS

PREP TIME: 15 MINUTES, PLUS 30 MINUTES TO 1 HOUR TO CHILL • **COOK TIME:** 30 MINUTES

Cake pops are a relatively new concept. They were invented in 2008, and I remember the first time I saw them at my local coffee shop—I was dumbfounded to discover that these little "lollipops" were made of cake. As a huge cake lover, I had to try one. It was honestly the greatest thing I'd ever tasted, and I loved how portable it was. When I learned how to make cake pops myself, I found that they're just as easy to make as they are delicious.

MAKES 38 CAKE POPS

One 15.25-ounce (432g) boxed cake mix, your choice of flavor

1 cup water

⅓ cup vegetable oil

3 large eggs

¾ cup prepared frosting, your choice of flavor

12 ounces (340g) candy melts, your choice of flavor

2 teaspoons nonpareils, your choice (optional)

SPECIAL EQUIPMENT

38 lollipop sticks

1. Preheat the oven to 350°F (180°C).
2. In a large bowl, whisk together the boxed cake mix, water, vegetable oil, and eggs until fully combined
3. Pour the cake mix into an 8x8-inch (20x20cm) baking pan lined with parchment paper and bake for 30 minutes or until a toothpick inserted in the center comes out clean.
4. Remove the cake from the oven and allow it to fully cool, then place it into a large bowl and crumble it well using your hands.
5. Add the frosting to the bowl with the crumbled cake and mix well with your hands.
6. Take about 1 tablespoon of the cake mixture, roll it into a roughly 1-inch (2.5cm) ball with your hands, and place it on a baking sheet lined with parchment paper. Repeat until you have about 38 cake balls.
7. Place the baking sheet in the freezer for about 30 minutes or in the fridge for about 3 hours.
8. Once the cake balls are almost set, prepare the candy coating. In a small micowave-safe bowl, add the candy melts. Microwave them in 30-second intervals, stirring frequently between intervals, until fully melted.
9. Remove the baking sheet from the freezer or fridge, dip the tip of a lollipop stick in the melted candy coating, and then insert it about halfway into a cake ball and place back on the baking sheet. Repeat with the remaining balls.
10. Dip the cake pops into the melted candy coating until all are fully covered. If using, add some nonpareils to the cake pops while the coating is still soft. Let the cake pops sit for about 5 minutes until the coating sets.

MONKEY BREAD

PREP TIME: 8 MINUTES • **COOK TIME:** 35 MINUTES

This is probably one of the easiest recipes in this entire cookbook. It's flaky, buttery, sweet, and just overall the perfect dessert. Most of the ingredients can be found in your pantry, and anyone can make it. I always used to buy premade monkey bread from the store, but now I just rely on this delicious recipe!

MAKES 1 BOWL

One 6-ounce (170g) can flaky layer biscuits (such as Pillsbury)

2 tablespoons granulated sugar

1 teaspoon ground cinnamon

2 tablespoons butter, melted

2 tablespoons brown sugar

1. Cut each biscuit into 4 triangular pieces.
2. In a medium bowl, mix the sugar and cinnamon. Add the cut biscuit pieces to the bowl and toss until fully coated.
3. Add the coated biscuits to a 6-inch (15cm) ovensafe saucepan or ramekin.
4. Preheat the oven to 375°F (190°C).
5. In a small bowl, mix the melted butter and brown sugar. Pour the butter and sugar mixture over the biscuits.
6. Bake the biscuits for 25 to 35 minutes until deeply brown in color.
7. Remove the biscuits from the oven and let cool for 5 to 10 minutes before serving.

NOTE

Consider adding a scoop of ice cream on top of the monkey bread to get that perfect hot-and-cold combination.

MINI CHEESECAKE CUPS

PREP TIME: 15 MINUTES, PLUS 20 MINUTES TO REFRIGERATE • **FREEZE TIME:** 30 MINUTES

Making a whole cheesecake requires a lot of effort, and it often ends up being too much. Most cheesecake recipes make a giant cake that's hard to finish, so a lot of it can go to waste. Here's a super easy, minimal-effort way to make cheesecake cups that satisfy your craving while saving you time and money!

MAKES 4 SERVINGS

2½ sheets graham crackers, 10 crackers

1 tablespoon butter, melted

1 cup cream cheese

½ cup heavy cream

1 teaspoon vanilla extract

¼ cup granulated sugar

2 strawberries, halved (or other berry of choice)

SPECIAL EQUIPMENT

2½-inch (6.5cm) paper baking cups

1. Place the graham crackers in a blender and blitz until you have fine crumbs.
2. Transfer the crumbs to a small bowl, add the melted butter, and mix until fully combined.
3. Place four paper baking cups into a muffin pan. Spoon the graham cracker mixture evenly into the cups and press down with a spoon to create a firm crust. Place the muffin pan in the fridge for about 20 minutes to set.
4. Meanwhile, in a medium bowl, combine the cream cheese, heavy cream, vanilla extract, and sugar. Whisk until the mixture becomes smooth and creamy.
5. Remove the muffin pan from the fridge and spoon the cream cheese mixture on top of the chilled graham cracker crusts, filling each baking cup to the top. Smooth out the tops with the back of a spoon.
6. Place the cheesecake cups in the freezer for 15 to 20 minutes, or until firm.
7. Before serving, top each cheesecake cup with a halved strawberry or another berry of choice.

COFFEE-CHOCOLATE PUDDING CAKE

PREP TIME: 15 MINUTES, PLUS 3 HOURS TO CHILL • **COOK TIME:** 2 MINUTES

Creamy, soft, decadent chocolate pudding cake is something you'll want to indulge in. The smooth and buttery quality of this pudding cake is easy and quick to achieve with just a few ingredients. This recipe doesn't require any fancy tools and is perfect for satisfying that sweet tooth.

MAKE 2 SERVINGS

- 1 egg yolk
- 1 tablespoon granulated sugar
- ½ cup coffee, prepared however you like it
- ½ cup dark chocolate chips
- Cocoa powder, for serving (optional)

1. In a small bowl, mix together the egg yolk, sugar, and coffee.
2. Place the mixture in the microwave and cook for 1 to 2 minutes, checking every 30 seconds until the mixture slightly thickens.
3. Add the dark chocolate chips to the mixture and let sit for 1 minute before mixing well.
4. Pour the mixture into a 3½-inch (9cm) ramekin and place it in the freezer for at least 3 hours until fully set.
5. Dust with cocoa powder before serving, if using, and enjoy it straight from the ramekin.

OREO MOLTEN CAKE

PREP TIME: 20 MINUTES • **COOK TIME:** 1 HOUR

If you don't already know, I am a huge fan of cakes. They are so easy to make; they can feed an entire party; and there are so many different kinds. For example, this unique molten cake spews out chocolate when you cut into it. It can definitely get messy, but you basically get a delicious chocolate fountain dip to enjoy with each bite!

MAKES 8 SERVINGS

Two 13.29-ounce (377g) packages Oreo chocolate sandwich cookies (about 66 cookies)

2½ teaspoons baking powder

2½ cups milk

2 cups semi-sweet chocolate chips

2 cups hot heavy cream

Chocolate sprinkles, for garnish (optional)

SPECIAL EQUIPMENT

Blender or food processor

1. Preheat the oven to 350°F (180°C).
2. Use a blender to crumble the sandwich cookies.
3. Transfer the crumbled cookies to a large bowl and add in the baking powder and milk. Mix together until well incorporated.
4. Pour the mixture into an 8-cup Bundt pan and bake for 55 to 60 minutes and then remove from the oven and set aside to cool for 10 minutes.
5. Meanwhile, make the ganache by melting the chocolate and placing it into a large bowl and pouring the hot heavy cream over the top. Let it sit for 1 minute and then mix until well combined.
6. Invert the cake onto a serving plate and pour 1 cup of the ganache over top of the cake. Let it rest until the ganache sets, then pour the remaining ganache into the empty center of the cake.
7. Add some chocolate sprinkles over the top, if using, and then serve immediately.

JAPANESE FLUFFY CAKE

PREP TIME: 15 MINUTES, PLUS 30 MINUTES TO COOL • **COOK TIME:** 1 HOUR

I love making this cake because it uses only a few ingredients but packs so much flavor. This recipe is one of my favorites, and it's a crowd favorite due to its perfect balance of sweetness. The light, moist texture and rich taste make it ideal for any occasion, whether it's a casual get-together or a special celebration. It's incredibly simple to prepare yet always impresses guests with its delightful taste and presentation.

MAKES 1 CAKE

- 3 egg yolks
- 1 cup vanilla yogurt
- 6 tablespoons all-purpose flour
- ½ teaspoon salt
- 3 egg whites
- ½ cup granulated sugar
- Powdered sugar, for garnish

SPECIAL EQUIPMENT

- Hand mixer
- 7-inch (18cm) circular springform pan

1. Preheat the oven to 300°F (150°C).
2. In a large bowl, add the egg yolks, yogurt, flour, and salt. Mix until the mixture thickens.
3. In a separate large bowl, add the egg whites and, using a hand mixer, start whisking them while gradually adding the sugar. Keep whisking until soft peaks form.
4. Combine the egg yolk mixture with the egg whites and gently mix them together.
5. Pour the combined egg mixture into a 7-inch (18cm) circular springform pan.
6. Place the springform pan into a 9x13-inch (23x33cm) rectangular baking pan and pour in boiling water until it fills the rectangular pan halfway (see Note).
7. Bake the cake for 1 hour, until a toothpick inserted in the center comes out clean.
8. Remove the cake from the oven and let the cake cool until it reaches room temperature.
9. Remove the cake from the springform pan and dust the top with powdered sugar before serving.

NOTE

The large rectangular baking dish just needs to be big enough to fit the 7-inch (18cm) springform pan inside.

TINY PANCAKES

PREP TIME: 5 MINUTES • **COOK TIME:** 15 MINUTES

Yeah, you can make regular pancakes, but that's so boring! Tiny pancakes look adorable, plus they're easier and less messy to make than regular pancakes. With just four ingredients (plus toppings), you can have the cutest, tastiest pancakes ever.

MAKES 1–2 SERVINGS

- 2 large eggs
- 9 tablespoons cake flour
- 2 tablespoons milk
- 1 teaspoon baking powder
- Butter, for serving
- Syrup, for serving

SPECIAL EQUIPMENT

Food-safe plastic squeeze bottle (see Note)

1. In a small bowl, add the eggs, cake flour, milk, and baking powder and mix well to combine (see Variation).
2. Place the mixture inside a plastic squeeze bottle. Place a large nonstick skillet over medium-low heat and then squeeze out the batter to make the tiny pancakes of your preferred size.
3. Let the pancakes cook for about 2 minutes, then flip and cook the other side for the same amount of time.
4. Transfer the cooked tiny pancakes to a bowl or plate, add a slice of butter on top, and drizzle with syrup.

NOTE

If you don't have a plastic squeeze bottle, use a spoon to scoop and dollop the mixture onto the pan.

VARIATION

The pancake batter doesn't have any sugar in it because the syrup will bring the sweetness. If you want sweeter pancakes, add 1 or 2 tablespoons granulated sugar to the batter.

NUTELLA BRIOCHE

PREP TIME: 30 MINUTES, PLUS 1 HOUR AND 30 MINUTES TO RISE • **COOK TIME:** 40 MINUTES

Nutella, a chocolate-hazelnut spread, is one of those products that was always in my house growing up. My family loved it, and we would often simply have it with some bread. This recipe transforms the idea of spreading Nutella on your bread into something extraordinary. The decadent flavor and silky texture of fresh brioche stuffed with Nutella should be illegal, but luckily for all of us, it isn't—and it's insanely delicious.

MAKES 3 SERVINGS

2 cups all-purpose flour, plus more for work surface

3 tablespoons granulated sugar

2¼ teaspoons instant yeast

4 tablespoons butter

½ cup milk, warmed to about 92°F (33°C)

1 teaspoon salt

3 tablespoons Nutella, divided

1 large egg

1. In a medium bowl, combine the flour, sugar, yeast, butter, and milk. Mix until a dough forms.

2. Lightly flour a work surface and your hands and knead the dough for 10 to 15 minutes until it becomes super soft. Place the dough in a bowl, cover with a clean dish towel, and let it sit at room temperature for 1 hour or until it doubles in size (see Note).

3. When the dough has risen, divide it into three pieces of equal size.

4. On a lightly floured surface, roll each piece of dough into a rectangular shape 6 inches (15cm) long and spread 1 tablespoon Nutella over the top third of the short side of the dough. Fold the Nutella-covered dough toward the center to cover it fully and gently press it shut. Use a knife to cut small vertical slices on the remaining third of dough, taking care to leave the edges intact. Fold the cut dough over the top of the Nutella-filled pocket. Repeat this process with the remaining two pieces of dough.

5. Place the three filled dough pieces side by side in an 8-inch (20cm) square cake pan, cover with the clean dish towel, and let sit at room temperature for 30 minutes more. Meanwhile, preheat the oven to 350°F (180°C).

6. In a small bowl, whisk the egg. After the dough is finished resting, remove the towel and brush the beaten egg over the tops of the dough.

7. Bake for about 35 to 45 minutes until golden brown and serve.

NOTE
To help your dough rise more efficiently, you can place the covered bowl with the dough ball in the oven, turned off but with the light on. This creates a warm environment that helps the yeast thrive.

JENGA CAKE

PREP TIME: 20 MINUTES, PLUS 30 MINUTES TO FREEZE • **ASSEMBLE TIME:** 1 HOUR, PLUS 1 HOUR TO CHILL

This recipe is definitely the most fun one in this entire book because you can actually play with it. I was always told not to play with my food when I was younger, so I made this recipe to fulfill my childhood dreams. This is basically a cake pop but in another form. It's really easy to make, and it's definitely a conversation starter at parties.

MAKES 40-50 CAKE BARS

1 plain 7-inch (18cm) unfrosted cake, your choice of flavor

¼ cup cream cheese

1 cup white chocolate candy melts (see Notes)

½ cup milk chocolate candy melts (see Note)

SPECIAL EQUIPMENT

40-50 cavity Jenga silicone mold (see Notes)

1. Crush the cake up with your hands until it's in small bits. Add the crushed cake to a large bowl, add the cream cheese, and mix until it reaches a doughlike consistency.

2. Pack the mixture into the Jenga mold and freeze for 30 minutes.

3. Place the white and milk chocolate candy melts into a medium microwave-safe bowl and microwave in 30-second intervals, stirring between intervals, until fully melted. Then give it a good mix.

4. Remove the mold from the freezer and remove the cake sticks from the mold.

5. Pour a little of the melted candy coating into a few mold cavities until the bottom is covered in a thin layer, then press the frozen cake sticks back into the mold. Repeat until all cake sticks are back in the mold.

6. Pour more melted candy coating over the top of the cake pieces. (You may need to remelt your candy coating if it begins to set.)

7. Place the mold in the fridge for about 1 hour to set before removing the coated cake pieces from the mold, assembling your tower, and serving.

NOTES

- Be sure to use candy melts and not actual chocolate for this recipe. Using candy melts allows the candy shell to be stable enough to hold its shape when coming out of the mold.

- You can find a few options online if you search for "Jenga silicone mold." A mold with rectangular bar shapes closest to 2.8x0.9x0.4 inches (7.1x2.2x1cm) will work best.

VARIATION

If you can't find an unfrosted cake or prefer to make your own, feel free to use a boxed cake mix, prepared per the package instructions.

ÉCLAIR CAKE

PREP TIME: 20 MINUTES, PLUS 3 HOURS TO CHILL • **COOK TIME:** 30 MINUTES

Éclairs are one of the best desserts in French pastry. They're perfect with their crunchy pastry, creamy filling, and chocolate topping. This éclair in cake form requires no baking and tastes just like my favorite French dessert, but there's more of it to go around!

MAKES 8 PIECES

6 large eggs

1 cup granulated sugar

5 cups milk, divided

3 tablespoons cornstarch

65-70 vanilla cookies (Nilla Wafers preferred)

2 cups heavy whipping cream

2 cups semi-sweet chocolate chips

1. In a large bowl, mix together the eggs and sugar and then set aside.

2. In a large pot placed over medium-low heat, add 4 cups milk and the cornstarch and bring to a light simmer.

3. Gradually pour the simmered milk into the egg mixture while whisking continuously.

4. Pour the mixture back into the pot and place it back over medium-low heat. Keep stirring the mixture until it thickens and becomes creamy. Once it reaches a thick, creamy consistency, turn off the heat and let the cream filling cool to room temperature.

5. In a separate large bowl, pour in the remaining 1 cup milk and dip the cookies in the milk. Then arrange half of the dipped cookies in a single, even layer in a 9x13-inch (23x33cm) baking dish.

6. Add a layer of the cream mixture over the top of the cookies and, using a spatula, spread it evenly. Repeat this process with the remaining cookies and cream, for a total of 2 layers.

7. Place the dish in the fridge and refrigerate for at least 3 hours.

8. Once the éclair is fully chilled, make the chocolate topping. In a medium saucepan over medium-low heat, bring the heavy cream to a light boil.

9. Place the chocolate chips into a large bowl, pour the warm heavy cream over them, and let it sit for about 1 minute. With a spatula, mix everything together until well combined.

10. Remove the éclair cake from the fridge and pour the melted chocolate over top. Return the cake to the fridge to allow it to set, then slice and serve.

GOLF BALL CAKE

PREP TIME: 30 MINUTES, PLUS 15 MINUTES TO CHILL • **COOK TIME:** 1 HOUR

Hyperrealistic cakes are impressive, but they usually require a ton of skill and experience to pull of successfully. I've found the cheat code for creating golf ball look-alikes by using a graham cracker cake base, chocolate melts, and a silicone mold. These simple cakes are easy to make, and will definitely make you seem like a baking genius to all your friends and family.

MAKES 12 GOLF BALL CAKES

23 sheets graham crackers

2 teaspoons baking powder

1½ cups milk

1 cup white chocolate candy melts (see Notes)

SPECIAL EQUIPMENT

High-speed blender

Two 12-cavity golf ball–shape silicone molds (see Notes)

Small food-safe brush

1. Preheat the oven to 350°F (180°C).
2. Place the graham crackers into a blender and blitz until fully crushed.
3. In a large bowl, combine the blended graham crackers, baking powder, and milk. Whisk until well combined.
4. Pour the mixture into a 9-inch (23cm) square baking pan and bake for 1 hour, until you have a graham cracker cake and a toothpick in the center comes out clean. Remove from the oven and set aside to cool completely.
5. Place the white chocolate candy melts into a medium microwave-safe bowl and microwave it in 30-second intervals, stirring between intervals, until fully melted.
6. Pour the melted candy coating into the two golf ball molds, spreading it evenly in each cavity with a small brush, creating a candy shell. Place the mold in the fridge for at least 15 minutes to allow the coating to firm up.
7. Using your hands, crush the entire cake in the pan, until it turns into crumbs.
8. Remove the golf ball molds from the fridge and carefully remove the candy golf ball halves. Fill the candy-shell halves with the crumbled cake. Be sure to carefully and firmly pack the cake into the candy shells.
9. To assemble the golf balls, slightly melt the edges of the filled candy shell on a warmed pan and then press the halves together. Repeat with all remaining cake-filled golf ball candy halves.

NOTES

- Be sure to use white chocolate candy melts, not actual white chocolate in this recipe. Using candy melts allows the candy to be stable enough to hold its shape when coming out of the mold.
- For the golf ball mold, you can find a few options online if you search for "golf ball silicone mold." Just make sure to find one with 12 cavities.

VARIATION

If preferred, boxed cake mix works as a great substitute for the graham cracker cake in this recipe. If using a boxed cake mix, prepare the cake per package instructions and begin the recipe at step 5.

ONE-PAN CHOCOLATE CAKE

PREP TIME: 10 MINUTES • **COOK TIME:** 20 MINUTES, PLUS 30 MINUTES TO CHILL

Baking an entire cake can be a messy and time-consuming process. You typically need multiple bowls, a baking pan, and several utensils. This one-pan chocolate cake eliminates all that and doesn't even require an oven—yes, you read that correctly, no oven! Everything is made in one pan; it's baked on your stovetop; and you'll have a clean kitchen. Baking a cake has never been easier.

MAKES 1 CAKE

- ¼ cup all-purpose flour
- 3 tablespoons cocoa powder
- ⅓ cup granulated sugar
- ¼ teaspoon baking soda
- 2 tablespoons butter, melted
- ¼ cup milk
- 1 large egg
- ½ cup heavy cream
- ½ cup semi-sweet chocolate chips, melted (see Note)

1. In a 6-inch (15cm) nonstick frying pan, whisk together the flour, cocoa powder, sugar, baking soda, melted butter, milk, and egg.

2. Cover the pan with a lid and place it over low heat. Cook the batter for 15 to 20 minutes until a toothpick inserted in the center comes out clean.

3. Meanwhile, make the ganache by heating the heavy cream in a medium microwave-safe bowl. Pop it into the microwave for about 2 minutes and then add the melted chocolate chips to the cream and let it sit for about 1 minute before mixing until fully combined.

4. When the cake is done, pour the ganache over the top and place it in the fridge for about 30 minutes to set before eating.

NOTE
To melt the chocolate chips, place them in a small microwave-safe bowl and microwave in 30-second intervals, stirring frequently, until fully melted.

OREO CAKE

PREP TIME: 5 MINUTES • **COOK TIME:** 20 MINUTES

As you'll notice, I'm a huge fan of cakes because whenever there's a cake, there's a celebration, and that means everyone is in a great mood. I'm the one who brings the cake because a homemade cake is almost always better than a store-bought one. But making a cake from scratch can require hours of time and a dozen different ingredients, and who has time for that? So, I sliced it in half (no pun intended) and came up with this delicious five-ingredient chocolate cake recipe.

MAKES 6-8 SERVINGS

28 Oreo chocolate sandwich cookies

1 teaspoon baking powder

1 cup milk

½ cup semi-sweet chocolate chips

½ cup hot heavy cream

SPECIAL EQUIPMENT

Food processor

1. Preheat the oven to 350°F (180°C).
2. Add the sandwich cookies to a food processor and pulse until finely crushed.
3. Into a large bowl, add the crushed cookies, baking powder, and milk and whisk until well combined.
4. Transfer the mixture into an 8-inch (20cm) round cake pan and bake for 15 to 20 minutes.
5. Set the pan aside to allow the cake to fully cool.
6. Once the cake has cooled, in a small bowl, add the chocolate chips and pour the hot heavy cream over the top. Let it sit for about 1 minute before mixing well until the chocolate is fully melted and combined.
7. Remove the cooled cake from the pan and pour the warm ganache on top.

SPONGE CAKE

PREP TIME: 20 MINUTES • **COOK TIME:** 20 MINUTES

This is literally what it says: a sponge cake. It not only looks like a sponge but also tastes as good as any other sponge cake out there. Don't be fooled by its appearance—I know sometimes food made just for looks can lack flavor, but not this cake. It's so fun to serve at parties and events; people get a kick out of it. The best part is you can play a prank on them, and the reactions are priceless.

MAKES 3 SERVINGS

½ cup granulated sugar
8 tablespoons butter, melted
3 large eggs
1 cup all-purpose flour
½ teaspoon baking powder
2 drops green food coloring
3 drops yellow food coloring
1 tablespoon apricot preserves

1. Preheat the oven to 325°F (165°C).
2. In a medium bowl, combine the sugar, melted butter, eggs, flour, and baking powder and mix well until it reaches a batter consistency.
3. Scrape ⅓ of the cake batter into another medium bowl and stir in the green food coloring. Add the yellow food coloring to the remaining ⅔ of cake batter in the original bowl. Stir both bowls until the color permeates the batter in each bowl.
4. Scrape each bowl of cake batter into a separate 8-inch (20cm) square cake pan. Bake the green cake for 10 minutes. Bake the yellow cake for 20 minutes.
5. Remove the cakes from the oven, let the cakes fully cool, then remove them from the pans.
6. Spread the apricot preserves in a thin, even layer over top of the yellow cake. Place the green cake on top of the preserves and press gently to adhere the two layers.
7. To serve, cut the cake into three rectangles the size and shape of a kitchen sponge.

SPIRAL CROISSANTS

PREP TIME: 15 MINUTES • **COOK TIME:** 35 MINUTES

When these spiral croissants first came out, they took over social media. People loved how they looked, tasted, and even sounded. I tried to get some at a spot in Los Angeles where they were being sold, but the line was so long that I immediately turned around, went to the grocery store, and made a super simple three-ingredient version at home. They're delicious, but worth waiting in line for? You decide.

MAKES 2 CROISSANTS

One 17.3-ounce (490g) sheet puff pastry, thawed according to package instructions

¼ cup heavy cream

½ cup semi-sweet chocolate chips

SPECIAL EQUIPMENT

Two 4-inch (10cm) metal crumpet rings

Piping bag

1. Preheat the oven to 400°F (200°C).
2. Unfold the puff pastry and cut it across the shorter side into eight 1-inch (2.5cm) strips. Taking a strip at a time, roll four strips together into a spiral pattern to form a circle-shape croissant that's about 1-inch (2.5cm) high and 3-inches (7.5cm) in diameter. Roll the remaining four strips together in the same pattern to form the second croissant.
3. Line a baking sheet with parchment paper, place the spiraled puff pastries on the baking sheet, each inside a 4-inch (10cm) metal crumpet ring.
4. Place another equal-size baking sheet on top of the first baking sheet, with a heavy ovensafe pan on top of the second baking sheet. This will ensure the croissants hold a firm shape as they bake. Bake for 35 minutes, until golden brown.
5. Remove from the oven and allow the baked croissants to completely cool.
6. For the chocolate sauce, place the heavy cream in a medium pot over medium-low heat and bring to a slight boil. Add the chocolate chips and mix until fully melted and combined. Let cool slightly and then pour the chocolate sauce into a piping bag.
7. Punch a hole about 2 inches (5cm) deep in the side of each croissant.
8. Pipe the chocolate sauce into the croissants and overfill the hole so the sauce drips down from the side. Serve immediately.

JAPANESE STUFFED PANCAKES

PREP TIME: 15 MINUTES • **COOK TIME:** 15 MINUTES

Classic pancakes are pretty good to eat and simple to make, but I think it's time for an update. These Japanese Stuffed Pancakes are the perfect upgrade. They're soft, airy, and fluffy, and when stuffed with Nutella, they melt in your mouth, making regular pancakes feel boring and plain in comparison.

MAKES 2 SERVINGS

2 large eggs
¼ cup granulated sugar
⅓ cup milk
1 tablespoon honey
⅔ cup cake flour
1 teaspoon baking powder
4 tablespoons Nutella

1. In a medium bowl, whisk together the eggs, sugar, milk, and honey until well combined

2. Sift the flour and baking powder into the egg mixture and whisk to form the batter. Whisk until the batter is smooth and no lumps remain.

3. Heat a medium nonstick skillet over medium-low heat and pour in the batter ⅓ cup at a time to make four pancakes.

4. Top two pancakes with 2 tablespoons Nutella each and spread it out evenly.

5. Place one of the plain pancakes on top of each Nutella pancake and, if desired, pinch the edges together until you have 2 stuffed pancakes. Serve.

FLUFFY PANCAKE

PREP TIME: 30 MINUTES • **COOK TIME:** 45 MINUTES

This is a pancake lover's dream come true—a pancake so thick that it will have you questioning if it's a pancake or a full-blown cake. This is definitely the fluffiest pancake you'll ever have, and its airy, spongy texture comes from an unexpected ingredient—vanilla ice cream. It's perfect for sharing when you don't feel like making multiple pancakes for everyone.

MAKES 4 SERVINGS

1 pint vanilla ice cream, softened
2 cups pancake mix
1 cup milk
1 tablespoon butter
½ cup syrup, your choice of flavor

SPECIAL EQUIPMENT
Hand mixer

1. Preheat the oven to 375°F (190°C).
2. In a large bowl, add the softened ice cream and, using a hand mixer, whip it up for about 2 minutes until smooth.
3. In a small bowl, whisk together the pancake mix and milk.
4. Add the pancake batter to the large bowl with the whipped ice cream and whisk until well combined.
5. Pour the mixture in a lightly oiled Dutch oven or medium ovensafe pot with a lid. The pot should be at least 4 inches (10cm) deep and the batter should only fill the pot partway to allow for it to rise.
6. Cover the pot and bake for 45 minutes and then remove from the oven.
7. Transfer the pancake to a serving plate, place the butter on top of the pancake, and pour the syrup over top.

DONUT HOLES WITH CARAMEL

PREP TIME: 20 MINUTES • **COOK TIME:** 15 MINUTES

Making donuts at home is usually a long and tricky process. I've had many failed attempts trying to get the consistency and texture just right. But with this donut recipe I developed, it's a hundred times easier to make donuts without sacrificing texture or flavor. Pair it with caramel sauce, and devour the best donuts you've ever made.

MAKES 2-3 SERVINGS

1 cup self-rising flour
¾ cup plain Greek yogurt
3 cups frying oil
1½ cups granulated sugar, divided
¼ cup water
¾ cup heavy cream, room temperature
2 tablespoons butter

SPECIAL EQUIPMENT
Candy/deep-fry thermometer

1. In a medium bowl, mix together the self-rising flour and yogurt until a dough forms.
2. Cut out a small piece of the dough and, using your hand, roll it into a 1-inch (2.5cm) ball. Make sure to use additional flour if the dough gets too sticky. Repeat until all the dough has been rolled into balls.
3. Add the frying oil to a medium pot over medium heat. Heat the oil to 350°F (180°C), using a deep-fry thermometer to measure the temperature.
4. Prepare a plate with ½ cup sugar and set aside.
5. Fry the donut holes in the hot oil until golden brown, 3 to 5 minutes.
6. Remove the donuts from the oil, place on the prepared plate of sugar, and toss the donut holes in the sugar until well coated. Set aside.
7. Prepare the caramel sauce. In a medium pot, add the remaining 1 cup sugar and water. Place the pot over medium heat and let it caramelize without stirring. This will take 4 to 6 minutes.
8. Once the sugar turns a golden amber color, carefully add the room-temperature heavy cream. Mix it in until fully incorporated. (Be cautious as the mixture may bubble vigorously.)
9. Turn off the heat and add the butter. Stir until the butter is fully melted and the caramel is smooth.
10. Serve the donuts alongside the caramel sauce for dipping.

CHOCOLATE DONUTS

PREP TIME: 20 MINUTES, PLUS 1 HOUR TO FREEZE • **COOK TIME:** 15 MINUTES

For the chocolate lovers out there, this is a dream come true. It's basically a chocolate bomb with creamy, melty chocolate flavors that'll make you drool. This isn't your typical donut. There is no yeast, no dough—just chocolate with breadcrumbs, so it's super easy to make. The best part is you don't have to knead any dough (which I hate). Get ready to taste your new favorite treat.

MAKES 6 DONUTS

Two 4.4-ounce (124g) chocolate bars
3 cups frying oil
1 cup all-purpose flour
4 large eggs
1 cup breadcrumbs
1 tablespoon powdered sugar

SPECIAL EQUIPMENT

Silicone donut mold
Candy/deep-fry thermometer

1. Chop the chocolate bars into small chunks and place them in a small microwave-safe bowl. Microwave the chocolate in 30-second intervals, stirring frequently between intervals, until fully melted.

2. Pour the melted chocolate into the donut mold and place the mold in the freezer until the chocolate has frozen, about 1 hour.

3. Prepare three separate small bowls. Place the flour in one bowl, crack the eggs into the second bowl and beat them, and put the breadcrumbs in the final bowl.

4. Add the frying oil to a medium pot and place it over medium heat. Heat the oil to 360°F (185°C), using a deep-fry thermometer to measure the temperature.

5. Remove the mold from the freezer and the chocolate from the mold.

6. Dip each chocolate donut in the flour, then eggs, and then breadcrumbs until fully coated. Repeat the process a second time so each donut is dipped twice in each ingredient. Be sure to leave no portion of the chocolate uncoated. Place them on a baking sheet or wire rack.

7. Fry the chocolate donuts in the hot oil for 1 to 2 minutes. (Watch carefully so no chocolate seeps out.) Transfer the donuts from the oil to a serving plate.

8. Dust the donuts with powdered sugar and serve immediately.

CAKES, PIES & SWEET BREADS

CHOCOLATE CAKE WITH CHOCOLATE BAR

PREP TIME: 20 MINUTES, PLUS 30 MINUTES TO COOL • **COOK TIME:** 55 MINUTES

Baking a cake from scratch has always been challenging for me. The consistency is never the same. The various types of flour, butter, and even eggs you use can make the cake taste and feel different, so I set out to create not only an easy recipe, but one that will always be consistent. It doesn't get any easier than this. There's literally no frosting—instead, we use a whole chocolate bar, which elevates the cake to a whole new level!

MAKES 1 SMALL CAKE

28 Oreo chocolate sandwich cookies

1 teaspoon baking powder

1 cup milk

One 4.4-ounce (124g) chocolate bar (Hershey's preferred)

SPECIAL EQUIPMENT

Food processor

1. Preheat the oven to 350°F (180°C).
2. Using a food processor, finely crush the sandwich cookies.
3. In a medium bowl, add the crushed sandwich cookies, baking powder, and milk. Mix well until combined.
4. Pour the mixture into an 8x4-inch (20x10cm) loaf pan and bake for 50 to 55 minutes, until a toothpick inserted into the middle comes out clean. Remove the pan from the oven and turn the oven off.
5. Let the cake sit in the loaf pan for about 30 minutes, then carefully flip it out of the pan onto a small baking sheet lined with parchment paper.
6. Place the chocolate bar on top of the cake and put the baking sheet back into the still-warm oven until the chocolate bar is slightly melted, about 1 to 2 minutes. Keep a close eye on it to avoid overmelting the chocolate. You should still see the markings on the chocolate. Serve immediately.

DESSERT CUPS, ICE CREAMS, CHOCOLATE & MORE

OREO CREAM CUPS

PREP TIME: 20 MINUTES • **COOK TIME:** 3 MINUTES

It's no secret that I absolutely love and adore Oreo cookies. If you have watched any of my videos, you know I have an obsession with them. Not only are they probably the best cookies in the world, but they are a versatile ingredient when it comes to making desserts. These creamy layered pudding cups are so simple to make but have the best texture combination with the ganache, whipped cream, and crust. This one's a crowd favorite!

MAKES 6 CUPS

36 Oreo chocolate sandwich cookies, divided

5 tablespoons butter, melted

2½ cups heavy cream, divided

1 cup semi-sweet chocolate chips

SPECIAL EQUIPMENT

Blender/food processor

Six 9-ounce (266ml) clear plastic cups

Piping bag (optional)

1. Add 24 sandwich cookies to a blender and pulse until crumbled.
2. In a medium bowl, add the crumbled cookies and melted butter and mix well.
3. Place an equal amount of the cookie and butter mixture into six clear plastic cups and, using the base of another plastic cup, press down on the mixture to create a crust.
4. In a separate medium bowl, whip 1½ cups heavy cream until stiff peaks form. Place the bowl in the fridge to allow the whipped cream to firm up for 10 to 15 minutes.
5. Crumble 6 more sandwich cookies in the blender.
6. Remove the whipped cream from the fridge, add the cookie crumbles to the whipped cream, and mix well to combine.
7. Using a piping bag or a spoon, add an equal amount of the cookie whipped cream to each of the six cups. Return the cups to the fridge while working on the next step.
8. Heat the remaining 1 cup heavy cream in a small saucepan over medium-high heat until it begins to simmer. In a small bowl, add the chocolate chips and pour the hot heavy cream over the top. Let it sit for 1 minute before whisking well to combine.
9. Remove the cups from the fridge. Spoon equal amounts of the ganache over the cookie whipped cream in each cup.
10. Place a whole sandwich cookie on top of the ganache in each cup and serve.

CHOCOLATE FROM SCRATCH

PREP TIME: 7 DAYS • **COOK TIME:** 15 MINUTES, PLUS UP TO 24 HOURS TO SET

While traveling in Switzerland, someone told me I'd never tasted real chocolate. They explained that most American chocolate bars lack cocoa nibs and cocoa butter, essential for true chocolate. Checking stores in America, I found they were right. Determined, I tried making a true chocolate bar myself. The process was long but fun and interesting. Making your own chocolate is easy; it just involves a lot of waiting.

MAKES 1 BATCH

4 cacao pods (see Notes)

⅓ cup granulated sugar

1 cup cocoa butter, melted

SPECIAL EQUIPMENT

Wet-stone grinder or high-speed blender (see Notes)

Silicone mold in shape of your choice

1. Cut open the cacao pods and place the beans into a large bowl, cover with a towel, and let them ferment at room temperature for 7 days. Stir the cacao beans occasionally throughout the week.

2. Once the beans are fermented, preheat the oven to 400°F (200°C).

3. Place the fermented beans on a baking sheet and bake for 10 to 15 minutes, until they have fully browned and darkened.

4. Once the beans are baked, remove from the oven and allow them to cool to the touch. Then carefully remove the outer shells of the beans to expose the cacao nibs.

5. Use a blender or a wet-stone grinder to grind the cacao nibs until somewhat smooth. If using a wet-stone grinder, let it run overnight. (The longer it blends, the smoother it becomes.)

6. Add the sugar and melted cocoa butter to the blender or wet-stone grinder and mix until the nibs, sugar, and cocoa butter are fully incorporated.

7. Pour the chocolate into the silicone mold and allow it to cool and harden at room temperature. Serve.

NOTES

- If you don't have access to fresh cacao pods or just want to skip the fermentation process, you can use 1 to 1½ cups of cocoa nibs instead. This will give you the same base needed for the chocolate-making process. You can find both cacao pods and cocoa nibs online.

- If you're using a blender, the texture of the chocolate will be a bit different. The beauty of a wet-stone grinder is how finely it can grind the cocoa nibs. If you have one, I highly recommend using it over a blender.

TIRAMISU CUPS

PREP TIME: 15 MINUTES • **COOK TIME:** 5 MINUTES

This twist on tiramisu replaces the traditional ladyfingers with an ingenious cake-like layer made from graham crackers. Prepared in tidy individual servings and topped with a rich chocolate ganache, it's an easy way to indulge in this creamy, coffee-spiked treat.

MAKES 2 CUPS

½ cup crushed graham crackers

½ teaspoon baking powder

2½ tablespoons whole milk

2½ tablespoons brewed dark-roast coffee

1 cup heavy cream, divided

2 tablespoons granulated sugar

2 ounces (57g) mascarpone (see Note)

½ cup semi-sweet chocolate chips, plus more for optional garnish

SPECIAL EQUIPMENT

Hand mixer

1. In a medium bowl, add the crushed graham crackers, baking powder, milk, and coffee and mix well.

2. Divide the mixture equally into 2 microwave-safe 8-ounce ramekins and microwave them for 1 minute. Set aside.

3. With a hand mixer, whip ½ cup of heavy cream in a small bowl until soft peaks form. Then add the sugar and mix it in.

4. Add the mascarpone to the sweetened whipped cream and mix it in until the cream thickens and the mascarpone is thoroughly incorporated.

5. Divide the whipped mascarpone mixture equally over the top of the graham crackers in the ramekins.

6. In a microwave-safe bowl, add the chocolate chips and the remaining ½ cup heavy cream. Microwave it in 30-second intervals, stirring between intervals, until fully melted.

7. Pour the melted chocolate equally on top of each of the ramekins of cream and sprinkle with chocolate chips or shaved chocolate, if using.

NOTE

If you can't find any mascarpone at the grocery store, you can always use cream cheese, but keep in mind that the texture will be a bit different. It still tastes amazing, I promise!

CHOCOLATE CHIP COOKIE CUP

PREP TIME: 5 MINUTES • **COOK TIME:** 2 MINUTES

Who doesn't love a warm chocolate chip cookie with a cold glass of milk? Well, we can make one in a cup that takes about 1 minute! Making homemade cookies is fun, but it typically takes a while and requires a lot of ingredients. This recipe satisfies that cookie craving quickly—all you need is a microwave and a mug.

MAKES 1 CUP

- 1 tablespoon butter, melted
- 2 tablespoons brown sugar
- 1 egg yolk
- 2 tablespoons all-purpose flour
- 2 tablespoon semi-sweet chocolate chips, divided

1. In a small bowl, mix together the melted butter, brown sugar, and egg yolk.
2. Add the flour and mix well until fully incorporated.
3. Add in 1 tablespoon chocolate chips and mix well. Set the batter aside.
4. Place the remaining chocolate chips in a small microwave-safe bowl and microwave in 30-second intervals, stirring between intervals, until fully melted.
5. Pour half the batter into a microwave-safe 8-ounce ramekin or mug. Add the melted chocolate in the middle, then layer the remaining batter on top of the chocolate.
6. Place the ramekin in the microwave and cook for 45 to 60 seconds until the cookie has baked.

JELLY ROLL-UPS

PREP TIME: 15 MINUTES • **CHILL TIME:** 1 HOUR

Fruit Roll-Ups have been around for quite some time, and they're delicious, but have you ever tried Jelly Roll-Ups? This is for all the Jell-O lovers out there—it's a new, fun way to enjoy gelatin dessert. You can use any flavor you like, and when you mix it with marshmallow, it gives the gelatin a creamy texture that is so enjoyable.

MAKES 4 SERVINGS

One 3-ounce (85g) package gelatin mix, your choice of flavor

½ cup water

1 cup marshmallows

1. Lightly oil an 8-inch (20cm) square cake pan with cooking spray and set aside.
2. In a medium microwave-safe bowl, combine the gelatin mix and water and mix well.
3. Microwave the gelatin mixture for 60 seconds. Remove from the microwave and mix again.
4. Add the marshmallows to the bowl and microwave it once more for 60 to 90 seconds.
5. Remove the bowl from the microwave and give the mixture another mix until fully incorporated. Transfer the mixture to the prepared cake pan.
6. Place the mixture in the fridge for at least an hour to fully set.
7. Once set, carefully remove the gelatin from the pan and gently roll it up.
8. Slice the rolled-up gelatin into 3-inch (7.5cm) pieces and serve.

EDIBLE PLANT

PREP TIME: 15 MINUTES • **ASSEMBLE TIME:** 30 MINUTES

Is it cake or not? I love watching those videos of people making hyperrealistic cakes. It's so fun to watch, but making them is very difficult. You need serious training and skill to do it perfectly, which I admit I lack. However, I didn't let that stop me from making this fun edible plant. It's super easy to make—anyone can do it—and it will definitely fool some people. On top of all that, it actually tastes amazing!

MAKES 1 EDIBLE PLANT

½ cup chocolate candy melts
2 teaspoons unsweetened cocoa powder
½ cup heavy cream
1 tablespoon granulated sugar
2 Oreo chocolate sandwich cookies
1 fresh mint leaf with the stem

SPECIAL EQUIPMENT

One 12-ounce (360ml) paper cup
Food-safe brush
Hand mixer.
Rolling pin

1. Place the chocolate candy melts in a medium microwave-safe bowl and microwave it in 30-second intervals, stirring between intervals, until fully melted.

2. Pour the melted candy coating into the paper cup, swirl it around the sides, and then pour the excess back into the bowl, leaving the walls of the cup covered in melted candy. Keep the poured-out chocolate in case you need to redo this step to add another layer of chocolate and make the cup walls stronger.

3. Put the candy-coated paper cup in the fridge for 5 minutes to set.

4. Once the candy has set, carefully peel off the paper cup to reveal the chocolate cup. Carefully brush the chocolate cup with cocoa powder. (The cocoa powder is more for the realistic look rather than the taste.) Set aside.

5. In a medium bowl, combine the heavy cream and sugar. Then, using a hand mixer, blend until stiff peaks form.

6. With a large spoon, scoop the heavy cream mixture into the chocolate cup and set aside.

7. Prepare the sandwich cookies. Separate the cookie halves and remove the cookie filling by scraping it away with a butter knife and then discarding it (or eating it). Place the cookies in a sealable plastic bag and crush them using a rolling pin.

8. Sprinkle the crushed cookies over top of the cream-filled chocolate cup and then "plant" the mint leaf stem in the cream.

BROWNIE IN A CUP

PREP TIME: 5 MINUTES • **COOK TIME:** 3 MINUTES

Cup desserts are one of my favorite types of recipes to make. Not only are they super easy to prepare—most can be made in just a microwave—but they're also convenient when you want a single serving or multiple individual servings for guests. Their versatility is unmatched. This brownie cup doesn't lack any of the textures you might get from a regular brownie, and the chocolate topping makes the flavor rich and delicious.

MAKES 1 BROWNIE CUP

8 Oreo chocolate sandwich cookies, divided
¼ cup milk
½ teaspoon baking powder
¼ cup heavy cream
½ cup semi-sweet chocolate chips

SPECIAL EQUIPMENT

Blender/food processor.

1. Place 5 sandwich cookies in a blender and pulse until well crumbled.
2. Add the crumbled cookies, milk, and baking powder to a medium bowl and mix until well incorporated.
3. Pour the cookie mixture into a microwave-safe 8-ounce ramekin or mug and microwave for 1 minute until fully baked.
4. To make the ganache, place the heavy cream in a medium microwave-safe bowl and microwave it for about 1 minute until it gets very hot, then add the semi-sweet chocolate chips to the bowl and let it sit for about 1 minute before mixing it until fully incorporated.
5. Pour the ganache over the brownie and crumble the 3 remaining sandwich cookies over the top before serving.

3-INGREDIENT PEANUT BUTTER CUP FUDGE

PREP TIME: 5 MINUTES, PLUS 1-2 HOURS TO CHILL • **COOK TIME:** 5 MINUTES

Reese's Peanut Butter Cups are probably one of the most popular candies on the market, and there's no mystery why—they taste absolutely amazing. They were my favorite candy to get for Halloween when I was young and trick-or-treating. Here, I created the easiest Reese's-based fudge recipe I possibly could with only a few ingredients. It's smooth and velvety with a rich flavor that'll leave you wanting more.

MAKES 16 PIECES

One 14-ounce (396g) can sweetened condensed milk

1 cup Reese's Miniatures Milk Chocolate Peanut Butter Cups, plus more for optional garnish

1½ cups white chocolate chips

1. Add all the ingredients to a medium pot over medium-low heat and stir until melted and well combined.
2. Pour the mixture into an 8-inch (20cm) square baking pan lined with parchment paper. Garnish the top with additional Reese's Miniatures, if using.
3. Place the mixture in the fridge for 1 to 2 hours to set.
4. Once firm, slice the fudge into 16 equal-size squares and serve.

CHOCOLATE GANACHE BROWNIES

PREP TIME: 45 MINUTES • **COOK TIME:** 30 MINUTES, PLUS 1 HOUR TO SET

As a huge brownie lover, I'm always trying to level-up my brownies. My favorite way to make this perfect dessert even better? Add ganache on top! The creamy, soft, velvety texture of ganache on top of the moist and chewy brownie is an unbelievably amazing combination. After making this recipe, you may never go back to plain brownies again.

MAKES 9 BROWNIES

2 cups semi-sweet chocolate chips, divided

8 tablespoons butter

1 cup granulated sugar

½ cup brown sugar

3 large eggs

½ cup all-purpose flour

¼ cup cocoa powder

Pinch of salt

2 cups heavy cream

Sea salt, for garnish (optional)

1. Preheat the oven to 350°F (180°C).
2. In a large microwave-safe bowl, add 1 cup chocolate chips and the butter. Microwave them in 45-second intervals, stirring between intervals, until fully melted and combined. Set aside.
3. In a separate large bowl, add the granulated sugar, brown sugar, and eggs and whisk until fully combined.
4. To the egg mixture, add the flour, cocoa powder, and salt and give that a good whisk until the batter is smooth.
5. Gradually add the melted chocolate to the brownie batter and mix until fully combined.
6. Line an 8-inch (20cm) square cake pan with parchment paper. Pour the batter into the prepared pan and bake for 25 to 30 minutes. Remove the brownies from the oven and set the pan aside to fully cool before moving to the next steps.
7. In a small pot over medium heat, add the heavy cream and bring to a slight boil.
8. In a small bowl, add the remaining 1 cup chocolate chips and pour the hot heavy cream over the top. Let it sit for 1 minute before whisking well to combine.
9. Pour the ganache over the top of the cooled brownies and let it sit for 1 hour to set. Sprinkle sea salt over the top, if using. Slice into 9 equal-size brownies and serve.

VARIATION

To simplify this recipe, you can use a boxed brownie mix prepared according to the box directions and then simply make the ganache (starting at step 7) to top the cooled brownies.

MARSHMALLOW CHOCOLATE BAR

PREP TIME: 25 MINUTES, PLUS 5 MINUTES TO COOL • **COOK TIME:** 20 MINUTES

The idea of stuffed chocolate bars is such a fun concept, and the possibilities for what you can stuff them with are endless. I decided to make marshmallow-stuffed chocolate bars because the texture of marshmallow fluff combined with a snappy chocolate bar works so well. Plus, you can achieve the nostalgic feeling of sitting around a campfire by placing the marshmallow-stuffed chocolate on top of a graham cracker.

MAKES 4 BARS

⅓ cup water

¾ cup granulated sugar

3 egg whites

¾ cup corn syrup

1 cup semi-sweet chocolate chips

SPECIAL EQUIPMENT

Candy/deep-fry thermometer

Hand mixer

Chocolate bar mold

1. In a medium pot over medium heat, combine the water, sugar, and corn syrup. Using a candy thermometer, stir continuously until it reaches a temperature of 240°F (115°C) and then remove it from the heat.

2. In a medium bowl, add the egg whites and whip with a hand mixer until soft peaks form. Gradually add the syrup and keep mixing for 5 minutes more.

3. In a small microwave-safe bowl, melt the chocolate chips in the microwave at 30-second intervals, stirring between intervals, until fully melted.

4. Cover your work surface with parchment paper or paper towels. Pour some of the melted chocolate into a 6x3-inch (15x6.5cm) chocolate bar mold, reserving some chocolate in the bowl. Flip the mold over the parchment paper or paper towels to allow the excess chocolate to drip onto it. Then flip the mold right-side up.

5. Spread the marshmallow cream into the molded chocolate and then cover the marshmallow with the remaining melted chocolate. Place the chocolate mold in the fridge for a few minutes to cool completely before removing from the mold and serving.

IT'S SO EASY TO MAKE

DESSERT BURRITO

PREP TIME: 20 MINUTES, PLUS 1 HOUR TO CHILL • **COOK TIME:** 5 MINUTES

I love a good burrito. All of those delicious fillings wrapped up in a tidy tortilla—what a perfect invention! This recipe takes the genius idea of a burrito and turns it into an irresistible dessert. From the tortilla-style wrap to the filling, everything has a sweet twist. It's super fun to make, and it tastes absolutely amazing.

MAKES 1 LARGE BURRITO

1½ cups chocolate milk
2 eggs
1 cup all-purpose flour
1 cup heavy cream
½ cup granulated sugar
½ cup crushed Oreo chocolate sandwich cookies
1 tablespoon unsweetened cocoa powder (optional)

SPECIAL EQUIPMENT

Hand mixer

1. In a large bowl, mix the chocolate milk, eggs, and flour until well combined.

2. Pour ⅓ of the chocolate milk mixture into a large nonstick skillet over low heat and cook until bubbles form, then flip it and cook for an additional 30 seconds. Set aside the cooked wrap and repeat until you have three chocolate wraps.

3. Pour the heavy cream into a large bowl and use a hand mixer to whip the cream until stiff peaks form. Add the sugar and whip again until fully incorporated. Gradually fold in the crushed cookies using a spatula.

4. Lay the wraps vertically, slightly overlapping each other to create one large surface. Spread the cookies-and-cream mixture down the middle, leaving about a 2-inch (5cm) gap around the edges of the wrap.

5. Carefully fold in the sides of the wraps and then roll it into a large burrito from top to bottom.

6. Place the burrito, seam side down, on a plate and put in the fridge for at least 1 hour to chill and set.

7. Dust with cocoa powder, if using, before serving.

CHOCOLATE BROWNIE DISH

PREP TIME: 30 MINUTES, PLUS 30 MINUTES TO CHILL • **COOK TIME:** 25 MINUTES

This chocolate brownie dish has the most irresistible texture you'll ever experience. It's creamy, soft, and rich in flavor. If you're looking for a simple dish to make, you won't be disappointed with this recipe. It literally takes just five ingredients and is definitely a crowd-pleaser.

MAKES 3 BOWLS

3 cups crushed Oreo chocolate sandwich cookies

2 teaspoon baking powder

1½ cups milk

2 cups heavy cream, divided

1 cup semi-sweet chocolate chips

Chocolate sprinkles, for serving (optional)

1. Preheat the oven to 350 °F (180°C).
2. In a large bowl, add the crushed cookies, baking powder, and milk. Mix well until fully combined.
3. Evenly divide the batter into 3 oven-safe bowls or soufflé cups, each about 4 inches (10cm) wide and 2 inches (5cm) deep. Bake for 25 minutes, then set them aside to cool completely.
4. Spread the whipped cream evenly over the tops of the brownie cakes.
5. Spread the whipped cream evenly over the top of the brownie cake.
6. In a small saucepan over medium-low heat, cook the remaining 1 cup heavy cream until hot.
7. Add the chocolate chips to a medium glass bowl and pour the hot heavy cream over the top. Let it sit for 1 minute and then mix until fully melted and combined.
8. Pour the ganache over the tops of the whipped cream layers and place the brownie cakes in the fridge for at least 30 minutes to set.
9. Garnish with chocolate sprinkles before serving, if using.

OREO ICE CREAM BAR

PREP TIME: 10 MINUTES, PLUS 4 HOURS TO FREEZE • **COOK TIME:** 2 MINUTES

There's no excuse for why you can't make this recipe right now. I can confidently say this is the easiest recipe in the entire book. It uses just three utensils, and you even use the packaging the cookies come in, making the cleanup process minimal. It tastes like a mix between an ice cream bar and a snow cone—surprisingly, it's the best frozen treat you'll ever have!

MAKES 1 BAR

One 2.4-ounce (68g) sleeve Oreo chocolate sandwich cookies, 6 cookies

4 tablespoons milk

1 cup semi-sweet chocolate chips

1 tablespoon vegetable oil

¼ cup crushed peanuts

SPECIAL EQUIPMENT

1 popsicle stick

1. Crush the cookies in the sleeve before carefully opening the sleeve from one end.

2. Pour enough milk into the sleeve until all the crushed cookies are fully submerged, then put a popsicle stick in the middle and place the sleeve in a cup so it stands straight up. Put the cup with the upright sleeve in it in the freezer for at least 4 hours.

3. Once the bar has frozen, place the chocolate chips and oil in a medium microwave-safe bowl. Heat the bowl in the microwave at 30-seconds intervals, stirring between intervals, until fully melted. Add the peanuts to the melted chocolate and mix well.

4. Remove the frozen bar from the freezer. Pour the melted chocolate with peanuts into a tall cup and dip the ice cream bar in the chocolate until fully covered.

5. Place the chocolate-covered ice cream bar back in the freezer for at least 5 minutes to firm up before serving.

KOREAN ICE CREAM BAR

PREP TIME: 20 MINUTES • **FREEZE TIME:** 1 HOUR

The best part of traveling is trying unique local dishes. It's inspiring to see how different cultures cook, plate, and serve their food. On a recent trip to Korea, I tried a marshmallow-covered ice cream bar. It was so delicious, with the fluffy, toasted marshmallow on the outside and strawberry ice cream in the middle. If you can't make it to Korea, this easy at-home version is almost as good.

MAKES 1 BAR

6 regular-size marshmallows

1 ice cream bar on a stick, your choice of flavor

SPECIAL EQUIPMENT

1 clean, empty single-serve milk carton or 12-ounce (340g) paper cup (see Note)

Food torch (optional)

1. Place the marshmallows in a large bowl and heat in the microwave for 1 minute. Stir the heated marshmallows. You might need to microwave them a bit longer if they are still too thick to stir.

2. Pour the melted marshmallows into an empty milk carton and place the ice cream bar in the center of the milk carton until fully coated in marshmallow.

3. Place the carton in the freezer for at least 1 hour to chill.

4. Take the ice cream bar out of the milk carton and toast the marshmallow using a torch, if desired.

NOTE

Make sure your ice cream bar will fit inside the milk carton or cup you select. A tall plastic cup will also do the trick in a pinch.

EDIBLE CHOCOLATE CHIP COOKIE DOUGH

PREP TIME: 5 MINUTES • **COOK TIME:** 1 MINUTE

We're all guilty of sticking our hands into the cookie dough tub and eating it raw. But if you read the fine print, you should never eat unbaked cookie dough because the uncooked eggs and flour can upset your stomach and possibly expose you to salmonella. Luckily, there's an edible cookie dough recipe that has the perfect texture and is totally safe to eat. Now we can all relive our childhood memories!

MAKES 1 SERVING

6 tablespoons all-purpose flour
1 tablespoon brown sugar
2 tablespoons granulated sugar
2 tablespoons milk
1½ tablespoons butter, melted
Pinch of salt
2 tablespoons chocolate chips, semi-sweet or milk chocolate

1. In a medium microwave-safe bowl, add the flour and heat it in the microwave for 1 minute. (This will kill any potentially harmful bacteria.)

2. Remove the bowl from the microwave and add the brown sugar, granulated sugar, milk, melted butter, and salt. Stir until well combined and a cookie-dough consistency is achieved. If the dough feels and looks a bit too soft, add a little more heat-treated flour to get the consistency you want.

3. Stir in the chocolate chips and serve.

COOKIES AND CREAM CHURROS

PREP TIME: 20 MINUTES • **COOK TIME:** 15 MINUTES

When I went to the fair as a kid, I always reached for the churros. They are the perfect sweet treat with a crunchy exterior and a soft, airy interior. While regular churros are already amazing, I wanted to add my favorite cookie to them and make the experience even better—and oh boy, it doesn't disappoint.

MAKES 16-20 CHURROS

24 Oreo chocolate sandwich cookies

1 cup all-purpose flour

2 large eggs

5 tablespoons milk

3 cups frying oil

1 cup granulated sugar

One 14-ounce (397g) can sweetened condensed milk (optional)

SPECIAL EQUIPMENT

Food processor

Candy/deep-fry thermometer

Piping bag with a star tip

Heatproof tongs

1. Cut parchment paper into 20 strips, each about 4 inches (10cm) long and 3 inches (7.5cm) wide. Set aside.

2. Add the sandwich cookies to a food processor and pulse until finely crushed.

3. In a large bowl, add the crushed cookies, flour, eggs, and mil, and mix well until a paste-like consistency forms. Set the churro dough aside.

4. Add the frying oil to a large pot over medium heat. Heat the oil to 350°F (180°C), using a deep-fry thermometer to measure the temperature.

5. Place the churro dough in a piping bag fitted with a star tip and carefully pipe the dough onto the cut strips of parchment paper.

6. Place the churros with the parchment paper into the frying oil 3 to 4 at a time, to avoid overcrowding the pot. Using tongs, carefully remove and discard the parchment paper once the churros are in the oil.

7. Fry the churros for 3 to 5 minutes, then transfer them to a plate lined with paper towels.

8. Add the sugar to a plate and roll the cooked churros in the sugar until fully coated.

9. Serve up the churros with a side of sweetened condensed milk as a dip, if using, and enjoy.

VARIATION
You can swap the Oreos for another cookie of your choice for a flavorful variation of this recipe.

OREO ICE CREAM SANDWICH

PREP TIME: 30 MINUTES, PLUS 2 HOURS AND 20 MINUTES TO CHILL • **COOK TIME:** NONE

Ice cream sandwiches are the best of both worlds. You not only get delicious ice cream, but also a cookie along for the ride. If you think about it, it's basically another form of cookies and milk. So let's make the perfect ice cream sandwich using Oreos instead, because as we all know, it's the best cookie out there.

MAKES 6 SANDWICHES

54 Oreo chocolate sandwich cookies, divided and then crushed

10 tablespoons melted butter, divided

2 cups heavy cream

$2/3$ cup condensed milk

SPECIAL EQUIPMENT
Hand mixer

1. In a medium bowl, mix 22 crushed sandwich cookies and 5 tablespoons melted butter.

2. Place the cookie mixture in a 9-inch (23cm) square cake pan, spread it evenly, and gently compact it to make a solid crust. Place the pan in the fridge for 15 minutes to chill.

3. In a separate medium bowl, whip the heavy cream using a hand mixer until soft peaks form. Add the condensed milk and 10 crushed sandwich cookies and then gently stir by hand.

4. Remove the pan from the fridge, pour the cream over the cookie crust, and spread evenly. Place the pan in the freezer for 2 hours or until frozen.

5. Once the pan is frozen, repeat step 1, preparing another mixture of the remaining 22 crushed sandwich cookies and the remaining 5 tablespoons melted butter. Then remove the pan from the freezer and spread the cookie mixture over the top of the frozen cream, pressing down to make another crust. Place the pan in the freezer for 5 minutes to set.

6. Remove the pan from the freezer and take the ice cream sandwich out of the pan. Cut it into 6 equal-size pieces and serve.

CHOCOLATE CREAM CUPS

PREP TIME: 20 MINUTES • **FREEZE TIME:** 45 MINUTES

Whenever I have guests over, I want to impress them with a homemade dessert but avoid getting my kitchen dirty or using a ton of tools. That's why I love making these simple cream-filled chocolate cups—they're delicious, easy to make, and require only a few ingredients and minimal kitchen tools. You can make them ahead of time and pull them out just before serving.

MAKES 2 CUPS

1 cup chocolate chips, semi-sweet or milk chocolate

2 cups heavy cream

½ cup condensed milk

1 teaspoon vanilla extract

SPECIAL EQUIPMENT

Two 3.25-ounce (96ml) single-serve plastic cups (see Note)

High-speed blender

1. In a microwave-safe bowl, add the chocolate chips and microwave in 30-second intervals, stirring between intervals, until fully melted.

2. Pour the melted chocolate into two plastic cups and swirl it around until the chocolate coats all sides of the cups. Let any excess chocolate drip back into the microwave-safe bowl to avoid a mess.

3. Place the cups in the freezer for 10 minutes until the chocolate has fully hardened.

4. While the cups freeze, make the cream. To a blender, add the heavy cream and blend on high until it thickens into whipped cream. Add the condensed milk and vanilla extract and blend again until well incorporated.

5. Remove the cups from the freezer and pour the cream into the chocolate cups. Return the cup to the freezer for 30 additional minutes.

6. Remove the cups from the freezer and then cover the top with more melted chocolate. (You may need to reheat your chocolate in the microwave.) Toss the cups in the freezer one last time for 5 minutes or until firm. Remove them from the cups and serve.

NOTE

You can get a little creative with the size of cups for this recipe, although I find it easiest to reuse clean plastic gelatin dessert cups or pudding cups.

TIRAMISU

PREP TIME: 30 MINUTES, PLUS 12-24 HOURS TO CHILL • **COOK TIME:** NONE

Tiramisu is a masterpiece. You have creamy mascarpone mixed with coffee-soaked ladyfingers and coated in a light dusting of cocoa powder for a combination that is both flavorful and perfectly balanced. The version I make is, of course, a lot simpler than the traditional method because it has no eggs, making the process much easier without sacrificing any flavor.

MAKES 8 SERVINGS

- 2 cups heavy cream
- 1 cup granulated sugar
- 1 pound (454g) mascarpone
- 15 ladyfingers
- 2 cups brewed espresso
- 1 tablespoon cocoa powder

SPECIAL EQUIPMENT

- Hand mixer
- 2-quart round or oval serving dish

1. In a medium bowl, add the heavy cream and whip, using a hand mixer, until soft peaks form.
2. In the same bowl, add the sugar and mascarpone and mix with the hand mixer until well combined. Set aside.
3. Pour the espresso into a small, shallow dish.
4. Layer the tiramisu. Dunk each ladyfinger in the espresso and then place it flat into the serving dish. Repeat until you have one layer.
5. Spread half the tiramisu cream over the top of the ladyfingers. Repeat steps 4 and 5 once more to form two total layers. At this point, the tiramisu can be refrigerated for up to 12 hours (see Note).
6. Sprinkle cocoa powder over the top of the dish just before serving.

NOTE

You can chill this dish in the fridge up to 12 hours or overnight before sprinkling with cocoa powder and serving. Chilling tiramisu for at least a few hours can enhance the overall flavor.

HOMEMADE ICE CREAM

PREP TIME: 30 MINUTES • **FREEZE TIME:** 3-4 HOURS BUT VARIES BASED ON THE CONTAINER

Ice cream is one of the best foods on this planet. There are endless flavors to choose from, it's perfect in all seasons—yes, even in winter—and it's just so satisfying to enjoy. This super simple recipe doesn't require an ice cream maker, uses only four ingredients, and is so easy to make that you'll want to whip up a batch every week.

MAKES 2 SERVINGS

1 cup heavy cream

7 ounces (198g) sweetened condensed milk

1 teaspoon vanilla exract

10 Oreo chocolate sandwich cookies

SPECIAL EQUIPMENT

Hand mixer

1. In a medium bowl, beat the heavy cream using a hand mixer until soft peaks form. Add the condensed milk and vanilla extract to the bowl and mix again until fully combined.
2. Place the cookies into a sealable bag and crush them to your desired consistency.
3. Gently fold the crushed cookies into the cream.
4. Place the ice cream mix into any freezerproof container and place it in the freezer until completely frozen.

INDEX

A
active dry yeast, 17
all-purpose flour, 17
appetizers and finger foods, 21–58
    Cheese Balls, 21
    Cheese Donuts, 54
    Cheese-Stuffed Chicken Nuggets, 32
    Cheese-Stuffed Onion Rings, 22
    Cheetos-Seasoned Chips, 29
    Chicken Rings, 37
    Crispy Garlic-Butter Fries, 30
    Crispy Potato Rings, 26
    Fully Loaded Nachos, 49
    Homemade Cream Cheese, 25
    Homemade "Mozzarella" Cheese, 38
    Ketchup Chips, 53
    Microwave Mug Pizza, 41
    Microwave Potato Chips, 35
    Onion Rings, 42
    Pizza in a Pan, 50
    Potato Boat, 45
    Potato Cheese Sticks, 58
    Scalloped Potatoes, 57
    Sriracha-Honey Chicken Nuggets, 46
apple cider vinegar, 17
appliances
    food processor, 14
    hand mixer, 14
    high-speed blender, 14
    oven with broiler, 14

B
baking powder, 17
baking sheets, 14
baking soda, 17
barbecue sauce, 17
beef
    Fall-Off-the-Bone Beef Ribs, 99
    Lule Kabobs, 75
    Smash Burger, 88
    Street Tacos, 64
    Tender Beef Short Ribs, 63
black pepper, 17
blender, high-speed, 14
breadcrumbs, 17
breads
    Cheese-Stuffed Bread, 71
    Cheese-Stuffed Flatbreads, 84
    Pan Bread, 80
    3-Ingredient Flour Tortillas, 87
Brownie in a Cup, 159
brown sugar, 17
Bubble Shrimp, 72
burgers
    Smash Burger, 88
burritos
    Dessert Burrito, 167
butter, 17

C
cakes, pies, and sweet breads, 105–143
    Cake Pops, 105
    Chocolate Cake with Chocolate Bar, 143
    Chocolate Donuts, 141
    Coffee-Chocolate Pudding Cake, 110
    Donut Holes with Caramel, 138
    Éclair Cake, 122
    Fluffy Pancake, 137
    Golf Ball Cake, 125
    Japanese Fluffy Cake, 114
    Japanese Stuffed Pancakes, 134
    Jenga Cake, 121
    Mini Cheesecake Cups, 109
    Monkey Bread, 106
    Nutella Brioche, 118
    One-Pan Chocolate Cake, 126
    Oreo Cake, 129
    Oreo Molten Cake, 113
    Spiral Croissants, 133
    Sponge Cake, 130
    Tiny Pancakes, 117
candy/deep-fry thermometer, 14
canola oil, 17
cheese
    cheddar, 17
    Cheese Balls, 21
    Cheese Donuts, 54
    Cheese-Stuffed Bread, 71
    Cheese-Stuffed Chicken Nuggets, 32
    Cheese-Stuffed Flatbreads, 84
    Cheese-Stuffed Onion Rings, 22
    Homemade Cream Cheese, 25
    Homemade "Mozzarella" Cheese, 38
    Mac & Cheese, 79
    mozzarella, 17
    Parmesan, 17
    Potato Cheese Sticks, 58
cheesecake
    Mini Cheesecake Cups, 109
cheesecloth, 14
Cheese-Stuffed Bread, 71
Cheese-Stuffed Chicken Nuggets, 32
Cheese-Stuffed Flatbreads, 84
Cheese-Stuffed Onion Rings, 22
Cheetos-Seasoned Chips, 29
Chicharrones, 100
chicken
    Cheese-Stuffed Chicken Nuggets, 32
    Chicken Rings, 37
    Honey-Butter Fried Chicken, 66
    Hot Wings, 95
    Lemon-Pepper Wings, 76
    Lollipop Barbecue Wings, 92
    Orange Chicken, 68
    Sriracha-Honey Chicken Nuggets, 46
chili powder, 17
chips
    Cheetos-Seasoned Chips, 29
    Ketchup Chips, 53
    Microwave Potato Chips, 35
chocolate. *See also* dessert cups, ice creams, chocolate, and more
    Chocolate Brownie Dish, 168
    Chocolate Cake with Chocolate Bar, 143
    Chocolate Chip Cookie Cup, 152

Chocolate Cream Cups, 180
Chocolate Donuts, 141
Chocolate Ganache Brownies, 163
Chocolate from Scratch, 148
Coffee-Chocolate Pudding Cake, 110
One-Pan Chocolate Cake, 126

churros
   Cookies and Cream Churros, 176

Coffee-Chocolate Pudding Cake, 110

colander, 14

Cookies and Cream Churros, 176

cooking vessels
   baking sheets, 14
   Dutch oven or deep pot, 14
   medium and large saucepans, 14
   nonstick frying pan, 14

cornstarch, 17

cream cheese
   Homemade Cream Cheese, 25

Crispy Garlic-Butter Fries, 30

Crispy Potato Rings, 26

croissants
   Spiral Croissants, 133

cutting board, 14

D

dairy
   butter, 17
   cheese, 17
   eggs, 17
   milk, 17
   sour cream, 17

deep pot, 14

Dessert Burrito, 167

dessert cups, ice creams, chocolate, and more, 147–184
   Brownie in a Cup, 159
   Chocolate Brownie Dish, 168
   Chocolate Chip Cookie Cup, 152
   Chocolate Cream Cups, 180
   Chocolate Ganache Brownies, 163
   Chocolate from Scratch, 148
   Cookies and Cream Churros, 176
   Dessert Burrito, 167
   Edible Chocolate Chip Cookie Dough, 175
   Edible Plant, 156
   Homemade Ice Cream, 184
   Jelly Roll-Ups, 155
   Korean Ice Cream Bar, 172
   Marshmallow Chocolate Bar, 164
   Oreo Cream Cups, 147
   Oreo Ice Cream Bar, 171
   Oreo Ice Cream Sandwich, 179
   3-Ingredient Peanut Butter Cup Fudge, 160
   Tiramisu, 183
   Tiramisu Cups, 151

donuts
   Cheese Donuts, 54
   Chocolate Donuts, 141
   Donut Holes with Caramel, 138

dry goods
   active dry yeast, 17
   all-purpose flour, 17
   baking powder, 17
   baking soda, 17
   breadcrumbs, 17
   cornstarch, 17
   sugar (granulated, brown), 17

Dutch oven, 14

E

Éclair Cake, 122

Edible Chocolate Chip Cookie Dough, 175

Edible Plant, 156

eggs, 17

equipment
   appliances
      food processor, 14
      hand mixer, 14
      high-speed blender, 14
      oven with broiler, 14
   cooking vessels
      baking sheets, 14
      Dutch oven or deep pot, 14
      medium and large saucepans, 14
      nonstick frying pan, 14
   other tools
      candy/deep-fry thermometer, 14
      cheesecloth, 14
      colander, 14
      cutting board, 14
      mixing bowls, 14
      parchment paper, 14
      rolling pin, 14
      sieve/strainer, 14
      wire rack, 14
   utensils
      heatproof tongs, 14
      knife set, 14
      measuring cups and spoons, 14
      skewers, 14
      slotted spoon, 14
      spatula, 14
      whisk, 14

F

Fall-Off-the-Bone Barbecue Ribs, 83

Fall-Off-the-Bone Beef Ribs, 99

finger foods. *See* appetizers and finger foods

flatbreads
   Cheese-Stuffed Flatbreads, 84

flour, all-purpose, 17

Fluffy Pancake, 137

food processor, 14

Fred62, 49

fries
   Crispy Garlic-Butter Fries, 30

frying oil, 17

frying pan, nonstick, 14

fudge
   3-Ingredient Peanut Butter Cup Fudge, 160

Fully Loaded Nachos, 49

G

Garlic Noodles, 96

garlic powder, 17

Golf Ball Cake, 125

granulated sugar, 17

H

hand mixer, 14

heatproof tongs, 14

high-speed blender, 14

INDEX   **187**

Homemade Cream Cheese, 25
Homemade Ice Cream, 184
Homemade "Mozzarella" Cheese, 38
Honey-Butter Fried Chicken, 66
Hot Wings, 95
hyperrealistic cakes, 125, 156

I
ice cream. *See* dessert cups, ice creams, chocolate, and more

J
Japanese Fluffy Cake, 114
Japanese Stuffed Pancakes, 134
Jelly Roll-Ups, 155
Jenga Cake, 121

K
kabobs
    Lule Kabobs, 75
Ketchup Chips, 53
knife set, 14
Korean Ice Cream Bar, 172

L
Lagasse, Emeril, 10
lemon juice, 17
Lemon-Pepper Wings, 76
Lollipop Barbecue Wings, 92
Lule Kabobs, 75

M
Mac & Cheese, 79
mains, sides, and breads, 63–100
    Bubble Shrimp, 72
    Cheese-Stuffed Bread, 71
    Cheese-Stuffed Flatbreads, 84
    Chicharrones, 100
    Fall-Off-the-Bone Barbecue Ribs, 83
    Fall-Off-the-Bone Beef Ribs, 99
    Garlic Noodles, 96
    Honey Butter Fried Chicken, 66
    Hot Wings, 95
    Lemon-Pepper Wings, 76
    Lollipop Barbecue Wings, 92
    Lule Kabobs, 75
    Mac & Cheese, 79
    Orange Chicken, 68
    Pan Bread, 80
    Smash Burger, 88
    Spicy Peanut Noodles, 91
    Street Tacos, 64
    Tender Beef Short Ribs, 63
    3-Ingredient Flour Tortillas, 87
Marshmallow Chocolate Bar, 164
McDonald's, 32
measuring cups and spoons, 14
Microwave Mug Pizza, 41
Microwave Potato Chips, 35
milk, 17
Mini Cheesecake Cups, 109
mixer, hand, 14
mixing bowls, 14
Monkey Bread, 106
mozzarella cheese, 17

N
nachos
    Fully Loaded Nachos, 49
nonstick frying pan, 14
noodles
    Garlic Noodles, 96
    Spicy Peanut Noodles, 91
Nutella Brioche, 118

O
olive oil, 17
One-Pan Chocolate Cake, 126
onion powder, 17
onion rings
    Cheese-Stuffed Onion Rings, 22
    Onion Rings, 42
Orange Chicken, 68
Oreos
    Brownie in a Cup, 159
    Chocolate Brownie Dish, 168
    Chocolate Cake with Chocolate Bar, 143
    Cookies and Cream Churros, 176
    Dessert Burrito, 167
    Edible Plant, 156
    Homemade Ice Cream, 184
    Oreo Cake, 129
    Oreo Cream Cups, 147
    Oreo Ice Cream Bar, 171
    Oreo Ice Cream Sandwich, 179
    Oreo Molten Cake, 113
oven with broiler, 14

P
Pan Bread, 80
pancakes
    Fluffy Pancake, 137
    Japanese Stuffed Pancakes, 134
    Tiny Pancakes, 117
pantry staples
    dry goods
        active dry yeast, 17
        all-purpose flour, 17
        baking powder, 17
        baking soda, 17
        breadcrumbs, 17
        cornstarch, 17
        sugar (granulated, brown), 17
    meat and dairy
        butter, 17
        cheese, 17
        chicken, 17
        eggs, 17
        milk, 17
        sour cream, 17
    other staples
        barbecue sauce, 17
        frying oil, 17
        lemon juice, 17
        olive oil, 17
        potatoes, 17
        soy sauce, 17
        vinegar, 17
    seasonings
        garlic powder, 17
        onion powder, 17
        paprika, 17

pepper (black, paprika, chili powder), 17
salt, 17
paprika, 17
parchment paper, 14
Parmesan cheese, 17
pasta
   Garlic Noodles, 96
   Mac & Cheese, 79
   Spicy Peanut Noodles, 91
peanut oil, 17
pepper (black, paprika, chili powder), 17
pies. *See* cakes, pies, and sweet breads
pizza
   Microwave Mug Pizza, 41
   Pizza in a Pan, 50
pork
   Chicharrones, 100
   Fall-Off-the-Bone Barbecue Ribs, 83
potatoes
   Crispy Potato Rings, 26
   Microwave Potato Chips, 35
   Potato Boat, 45
   Potato Cheese Sticks, 58
   russet, 17
   Scalloped Potatoes, 57

R
Ramsay, Gordon, 57
ribs
   Fall-Off-the-Bone Barbecue Ribs, 83
   Fall-Off-the-Bone Beef Ribs, 99
   Tender Beef Short Ribs, 63
rings. *See also* onion rings

Chicken Rings, 37
Crispy Potato Rings, 26
rolling pin, 14
russet potatoes, 17

S
salt, 17
saucepans, medium and large, 14
Scalloped Potatoes, 57
seafood
   Bubble Shrimp, 72
seasonings
   garlic powder, 17
   onion powder, 17
   paprika, 17
   pepper (black, paprika, chili powder), 17
   salt, 17
short ribs
   Tender Beef Short Ribs, 63
sides. *See* mains, sides, and breads
sieve/strainer, 14
skewers, 14
slotted spoon, 14
Smash Burger, 88
sour cream, 17
soy sauce, 17
spatula, 14
Spicy Peanut Noodles, 91
Spiral Croissants, 133
Sponge Cake, 130
Sriracha-Honey Chicken Nuggets, 46
Street Tacos, 64
sugar (granulated, brown), 17

sweet breads. *See* cakes, pies, and sweet breads

T
tacos
   Street Tacos, 64
Tender Beef Short Ribs, 63
thermometer, candy/deep-fry, 14
3-Ingredient Flour Tortillas, 87
3-Ingredient Peanut Butter Cup Fudge, 160
Tiny Pancakes, 117
Tiramisu, 183
Tiramisu Cups, 151
tongs, heatproof, 14
tools (miscellaneous). *See also* equipment
   candy/deep-fry thermometer, 14
   cheesecloth, 14
   colander, 14
   cutting board, 14
   mixing bowls, 14
   parchment paper, 14
   rolling pin, 14
   sieve/strainer, 14
   wire rack, 14
tortillas
   3-Ingredient Flour Tortillas, 87

U
utensils
   heatproof tongs, 14
   knife set, 14
   measuring cups and spoons, 14
   skewers (metal or bamboo), 14

slotted spoon, 14
spatula, 14
whisk, 14

V
vegetable oil, 17
vinegar (white, apple cider), 17

W
whisk, 14
white vinegar, 17
whole milk, 17
wings
   Hot Wings, 95
   Lemon-Pepper Wings, 76
   Lollipop Barbecue Wings, 92
wire rack, 14

Y
yeast, active dry, 17

Acknowledgments

First and foremost, I want to thank my fans and supporters—none of this would be possible without you. Thank you for believing in me and trusting me. I am forever grateful for the position I'm in, and I will always keep you in my heart.

Thank you to my mom and dad, the two people who have always believed in me no matter what life has thrown my way. Your unwavering support throughout all my crazy adventures and your encouragement to never give up mean the world to me. I love you both more than words can express.

To my team: You guys deal with my crazy ideas on a weekly basis and have been instrumental in getting me to this point in my career. Your hard work and determination inspire me every day to do and be better.

To my life partner, Audris: None of this would have been possible without you. You were the reason my first-ever video went viral. You've stood by me through the ups and downs and the best and worst days, and you never stopped believing in me. Your motivation has kept me going, and I love you forever.

Thank you to my friends. You've been with me through it all—from the days when I was just a young boy to the person I am today. You've seen my progression and given me the encouragement I needed to reach this point. I'll always be grateful for you.

Finally, I want to thank the DK team for giving me the opportunity to write my first book. A heartfelt thanks to Brandon, Jessica, Max, Judean, David, Diana, Elle, and the wonderful folks behind the scenes who worked tirelessly to bring this book to life. I deeply appreciate your hard work and dedication to this project.

About the Author

Patrick Zeinali is an innovative food content creator out to prove to the world how simple cooking can be. He started his journey in 2019 with the goal of showing people how easy it is to make mouthwatering food at home with only a handful of ingredients. Over the years, he has entertained millions of viewers with his exuberant videos, honed his cooking skills, and developed many novel uses for his favorite cookie: the Oreo. He lives in Los Angeles.